DURGA PUJA

WITH NOTES AND ILLUSTRATIONS

PRATAPCHANDRA GHOSHA

BOOKS FOR ALL
DELHI-110052

Sales Office:
D K Publishers Distributors P Ltd.
1, Ansari Road, Darya Ganj,
New Delhi-110002
Phones: 3261465,3278368
Fax : 3264368

ISBN 81-7386-206-0

First Published 1871
First Published in **BFA** 1997

Published By:
Books For All
B-2, Vardhaman Palace,
Nimri Commercial Centre,
Ashok Vihar Phase-IV,
Delhi-110052
Phone: 7401672

Printed At:
D K Fine Art Press P Ltd.
Delhi-110052

PRINTED IN INDIA

PREFACE.

About a week before the Durga Puja holidays ensued I requested the author to write a paper on this chief national festival of the Hindus of Bengal, giving an account of the rites and ceremonies connected with it. He readily complied with my request, and although written at the spur of the moment and necessarily in great hurry, the paper has proved so interesting and has been so favorably received by the public that I have thought it proper to reprint it in the present form, chiefly with a view to circulate it among oriental scholars and others, who take interest in the religious institutions of the Hindus. The difficulties, which the author has met with in rendering into English the peculiar forms and expressions of Sanskrit Mantras and Slokas, may be easily imagined by those who have an experience of such work, and it is I think sufficient to mention that he has paid more attention to matter than to manner.

The Introduction and the Notes have been added by the author and the illustrations executed by Babu Tulsidas Pal, a student of the Government Arts School of Calcutta.

Calcutta,
The 18th December, 1871.

EDITOR,
Hindoo Patriot.

PREFACE

About a year before [illegible] [illegible] [illegible] [illegible] [illegible] [illegible] [illegible] the national festival [illegible] [illegible] of Bengal. [illegible] [illegible] of the [illegible] and [illegible] connection with [illegible]. The results compared with my [illegible] [illegible] [illegible] of the [illegible] and [illegible] [illegible] [illegible]. [illegible] is placed [illegible] [illegible] [illegible] favourably received by the public [illegible] [illegible] thought it [illegible] [illegible] in the [illegible] [illegible] [illegible] [illegible] used [illegible] in [illegible] and other [illegible] [illegible] [illegible] of the [illegible]. The difficulties [illegible] author has met with [illegible] [illegible] the [illegible] and [illegible] [illegible] and [illegible] many [illegible] imagined by those who have [illegible] of such [illegible] and [illegible] that [illegible] to [illegible] them to [illegible].

The Introduction and the Notes [illegible] by the author and the illustrations [illegible] by [illegible] of the Government Art School, Calcutta.

[illegible] [illegible]

[illegible] [illegible] 1971. [illegible] [illegible]

INTRODUCTION.

MODERN scholars have elevated comparative religion or mythology like comparative philology to a science, and in investigating the origin of the religious festivals and ceremonies of the ancients nothing perhaps strikes the student more forcibly than the reproduction of the same principles, the same thoughts, the same sentiments, and even the same forms in different climes and among different families of man. Thus Durgotsava, the chief religious festival of the Hindus, has its parallel among the Egyptians, the Chaldæans, the Assyrians, the Phœnicians, the Greeks, and the ancient Arabs.

In Lower Egypt and Phœnicia the ceremony or festival to Osiris or Isis (Adonis and Astarte) used to be observed for eight days at the commencement of Autumn when the sun entered the sign of Cancer. Theocritus describes the ladies of Syracuse embarking for Alexandria to celebrate the festival in honour of Adonis. Arisnoe the sister and wife of Ptolemy Philadelphus bore the statue of Adonis herself. She was accompanied with women of the highest station in the city holding in their hands basketsful of cakes, boxes of perfumes, flowers, branches of trees and all sorts of fruits. The solemnity was closed by other ladies bearing carpets &c. The procession marched in this manner along the sea-coasts to the sound of trumpets and other instruments accompanying the voices of musicians. They carried corn in earthen vessels which they sowed there together with flowers, springing grass, fruits, and young trees and Lettices, Suidas Hesychins &c.

Theophrastus informs us that at the end of the ceremony they used to throw those portable gardens either into a fountain or into the sea. This statement is corroborated by Eustatthius and the Scholiast on Theocritus. In the Hebrew scriptures these worshippers were called Dendrophori or tree-bearers, for they painted a tree on their body as Astarte, Ashtaroth, Aser meaning a tree or a grove. Macrobius says that this ceremony was diffused throughout Assyria. Lucian quoted by the Abbe Banier speaking of the temple of Hieropolis in Syria says that "in this sanctuary are two golden statues, one of Jupiter supported by oxen, and other of Juno by lions. The last is a kind of Pantheon that bears the symbols of several other goddesses. (Minerva, Venus, the Moon, Rhea, Diana, Nemesis and the Destinies). The animals sacrificed were the ox, the sheep and the goat." It should be remembered that Lucian was a Greek writer, and that he naturally saw Jupiter and Juno in the Osiris and Isis or Astarte, in the same way that Sanchoniathon and Porphyry call Baltis the Mistress or Queen of the heavens, the Isis of the Egyptians and the Allahat of the Arabs. The latter observed the festival of Allahat in autumn and that of Lat in spring. Kaushiki is a name of Durga, for she is said to be flower-formed, and Ovid elegantly describes the transformation of Adonis into a flower. In Hindusthan a similar Procession of ladies bearing twigs of trees, flowers, fruits and dishes and baskets and singing accompanied with the beat of musical instruments may still be seen on the occasion of the Dasahara festival; the same practice of sowing grains and of putting on the pagri (the head-dress) of men and in locks of hair of women the springing grass on the Vijaya Dasami day is still followed; and the same worship of portable gardens and the throwing of them at the end of the festival into a fountain or stream is still observed. The Vedas, though they ignore the adoration of any visible gods or tangible forms of modern Hindu idolatry, have sung of the Panchasaradiya Yajna and Vasantotsava or the autumnal and vernal festivals.* Not only this, but in the Aranyaka, a later appendage to the Black Yajur Veda, laudatory hymns are also given to invoke Amvika, another name for Durga. The Puranas likewise mention that in the month of Madhu agreeing with the modern lunar month of Chaitra and also in Isa agreeing with the modern lunar Asvina the Devi was worshipped.

But let us pause to enquire who this wondrous Devi is adored at the beginning of creation by Brahma the first-born of heaven for fear of the Titans (Madhukaitabha) and thence forward by man. Is she a deified heroine like Semiramis, or a remarkable historical personage like Lucretia, or a personification of natural object as Thetes or a creature of mere fancy and speculation like Ceres or Pallas, or the offspring of a chimera, the creation of an idle, terrified brain, a hob-goblin, a Siren, a Naiad or a Driad? Decidedly she is none of these, for a goddess so universally and contemporarily adored could not be the creature of fiction which is local in its very nature. What then could this prodigy riding on a ferocious lion be? She could not

* See "Hindoo Patriot," Oct., 25, 1869.

be Veritas, the goddess of Truth, subduing the lion by the force of her charms, for she is represented as a martial goddess in the act of fighting. But how could nature give birth to a monstrous being with ten arms and three eyes? We know of no history or philosophy that can reconcile this palpable absurdity and inconsistency in nature to aught of truth or fiction. Where must we turn then to find the true character and attributes of the Divinity. In Hindu mythology she is once described as Adya Sakti, Primæval Energy, Primum Mobile of the Gods, again she is said to be Sati, the daughter of Daksha, Cœlum, and next as the progeny of Himavat and consort of the Kailasian Siva, in which last attribute she is compared with the Olympian Juno, consort of Jove of the Greek Pantheon, and with Isis, Isi, the wife of Osiris, Isvara, of ancient Egypt, as also with the Holy Virgin, Alma-mater of Christian theology, with Allahat of the idolatrous Arabs, and with Astarte or Ashtaroth of the early Assyrians. Indeed, she is unanimously recognised by all idolatrous nations as the primary female copartner of the Eternal God, represented as the Adi-purusha, first male agent of creation. The idea of the co-existence of a co-eternal female co-partner of the male creator of the universe is not at all compatible with our intuitive knowledge of the Self-Existent God, though the Darsanas regard her as some conspicuous object in nature, for instance the Sankhyas call her Prakrti or Nature, the Naiyayikas, Adya Sakti or Prime Energy of the Deity, and the Vaidantias, Maya or Illusion. But why should Nature, Energy or Illusion be represented by the lovely form of a Virgin, made terrific with her rows of arms, triple eyes &c?

Or why should Nature our common mother, divine Omnipotence, be portrayed as waging everlasting war with Demons and not nursing her children with fostering care? And above all how such speculations seized the mind through the length and breadth of the ancient world and became the theme of the epics of poets of several nations and the beau ideal of the Deity of all.

We must it appears then seek to trace this universal Verego in something that is common to all?

Does she then reside in the heavens? The early Chaldæans and Phœnicians from their knowledge of the heavenly bodies fell at last to their worship. The Hindus as well as the other Arian nations have adored from time immemorial the heavenly luminaries as beings superior to man, and have from their supposed extraordinary influence adorned them with suitable attributes. In the heavens therefore we must seek for the Devi, for in the heavens we find the heavenly Virgin shining in full lustre and throwing light on the grand mystery of her origin. She proves at once to be the first female Divinity of heaven, the daughter of Daksha, progenitor of the Stars, the holy Virgin of the early Christians and the Astarte of the Assyrians. She proved verily to be the daughter of Himavat by Mena, the Manasasarovara, from her position over the eastern extremity of the mount, whence the declination to the southern course of the sun commences in his equatorial line of the Meru, and whence the constellation is seen to rise in early autumn evenings. To the left of the constellation Virgo and a little below it, is situated the constellation of the Centaur with its body of half buffalo and half man. On the other side of Virgo the heavens stands the constellation Leo almost as far removed from Virgo upwards as the Centaur is downwards; Virgo, Virgin, is the Devi, Centaur is the Demon Mahisasura, and Leo, the Devi's Lion.

Some have supposed her to be the planet Venus, the beauty of heaven, while others have taken her for the fair harvest moon of autumn; but the fixed lady Virgo can not be properly identified with these moving male luminaries of the Hindu Sastras. The moon is called the lord of stars (tarapati), while Venus is known as the beauty of the stars (tarasundari). The festival of the harvest moon takes place on the full moon of Isa (Asvina), but that of the Virgin commences on the pratipada, the first day after the new moon. It does not therefore appear reasonable to suppose her as identical with the moon from the epithet Umasasi or moon-like Uma by way of comparison.

Durga otherwise called Kanya or Kumari as has been premised above is identical with Virgo, the Zodiacal sign of the autumnal equinox in the solar month of September, reckoned as the initial moment of one of the Hindu system of years from the sun's progression or declination to the southern hemisphere, the region of the Demons. She is also the sign of the earth's position in the vernal equinox of Chaitra or more accurately Madhu, when the sun is situate in its opposite sixth sign of Pisces, which also divides the annual circle into two hexamensic periods. Hence the point of ascension of the sun from the southern to the northern hemisphere in the vernal equinox as well as that of his aescension or declination from the upper to the lower hemisphere constitute the beginning of the two equinoctial years of the Hindus and count as the periods for worshipping Virgo, Virgin, Kumari, the Devi. This two-fold division of the Hindu year with reference to the heliacal rising and setting of the constellation has its counterpart in the alternate predominance of darkness and light, night and day, in the diurnal revolution of the sun, to which the Dakshinayana and Uttarayana of the Hindu astronomer have been likened. In the diurnal revolution of the starry heaven the group of the three constellations Virgo, Centaur and Leo is almost invisible at night in autumn, and Kanya, Virgo, following upon Leo, the lion, obscures the next constellation Centaur by the brilliancy of the sun, to whom Virgo might be said to be married. It would not perhaps be too violent to suppose that the group of the three figures worshipped in the autumnal festival is the clay representation of the astronomical phenomenon of bright heavenly luminaries. But why should a similar group be worshipped in the spring season and why is the latter regarded as the older of the two season festivals ? Is it because the constellations of Leo, Virgo and Centaur are visible in the evenings of spring when the sun is in the opposite sign of the zodiac ? Such a supposition may be compatible with the present advanced state of astronomical knowledge, but how did the ancient Hindus, who had not made such progress in astronomy, seize the idea ? As the position of the sun in Virgo in autumn led to the autumnal festival, so the position of the earth, it might be supposed, in (Virgo) the sign opposite to Aries led to the revival of the same festival in spring. The festival in autumn continues for a period of ten days commencing from the first lunation after new moon,* but in spring it lasts only for four days ending on the tenth lunation from pratipada. The Autumnal festival again, though reckoned in the Sastras as the later of the two, is performed in a more elaborate manner than the Vernal. The year of the early Hindus commenced with the Vernal Equinox, and the signs of the Zodiac together with the constellations or groups of stars, which compose them, have their beginning according to Hindu calculation in the Vernal Equinox, the moment of the commencement of the sun's ascension to the northern hemisphere or the region of the gods; and the inhabitants of that hemisphere possibly thought of celebrating the festival in honour of Virgo at the time of the Vernal Equinox, which it might be supposed was in earlier days none other than *a*. Virginis. Owing to the retrograde motion in space of the solar system as regards its position in relation to the fixed stars, in other words, owing to the Precession of the Equinoxes the equinoctial points have gradually retrograded and changed places. In the hypothetical days when the sun was in the constellation Virgo the spring possibly prevailed, and when in Aries the autumn took possession of the earth.

Next, it might be asked whether the spring festival had the precedence of the autumnal, because in the ruder days of astronomical science the group of stars forming Virgo, visible in the evenings of spring, first attracted the notice of the observing, and suggested the idea of worshipping tangible representations of the same, and thus gave rise to the Vasantotsava or Vasanti Puja, which was first

* Jayasingha in his Kalpadruma states that the Vasanti-Puja should be performed from the pratipada to dasami.

instituted in honor of the Virgin. In later days the enlightened observers of the heavens and of the motion of the heavenly bodies discovered the more important phenomenon of the motion of the sun in the ecliptic, and found that the constellation Virgo, one of the many groups into which they had triangulated the space of the heavens, fell within the track of the sun. And having discovered this they fell upon the practice of worshipping Virgo at such a time when the most important luminary the sun was in it.

The Hindu constellation Virgo as being composed of Hasta, Chitra and a portion of Svati, consists of Corvus, Virgo, and Bootes of the Western astronomers. Hasta is identified with *a. b. c. d.* of Corvus, which is situated a little towards the south-west extremity of the constellation Virgo, and by calculation it has been determined that the Equator passed through it in B. C. 2350, the Equator of A. D. 560, however passed a little towards the north of Chitra, *a* Virginis.* In the autumnal festival therefore the bodhana or the arousing of the goddess Virgin *i. e.* the moment of the sun's leaving Leo in order to embrace Virgo should be commenced earlier. The Autumnal Equinox in A. D. 560, happened accordingly much closer to Chitra, the asterism proper of Virgo than in B. C. 2350.

The Puranas might have added the worship of the twin-stars Asvini, *b. c.* Arietis, the Castor and Pollox of the Greeks, in which the sun enters when the constellation Virgo commences to rise in autumn evenings. At the time these two stars were discovered they formed the asterism of the lunar mansion that is the junction of Isa (ancient Asvina)

* Burgess' Surya-Siddhanta.

and hence the month Asvina named after the phenomenon. Do these two represent the Kartikeya and Ganesa of the Bengal pratima of Durga, and does the twin star Bharani, for it is in the Vedas sometimes spoken of as the plural Bharanyas, represent Lakshmi and Sarasvati, as supporting (Bharana means to support) the corporeal and intellectual existence. But Bharani is figured as the Yoni or pudendum muliebre, and is formed as a triangle, the southernmost of which is the junction star and its divinity is Yama. It is therefore difficult to prove that the Puranas viewed it, against the text of the Vedas, only in its meaning of supportress, for the Puranas as a rule do not contradict the Vedas. Or do the two scales of Libra represent the twin sisters Lakshmi and Sarasvati. Or the latter the goddess of Krittika or more properly the Krittikas the six stars of the Pleiades, whose regent is Agni. The allegory could be pursued a little further, and the ten arms of Durga could be said to stand for the ten signs of the zodiac, which lie on both sides of the constellation. But is it not too much to suppose that the authors of the Vedas, who hymned the praise of the Autumnal and Vernal Festivals, were so intimately acquainted with the motions and positions of the heavenly bodies, when even the very names of most of them do not occur in their books? The Vedas present to evidence of even the existence of the system of asterisms, indeed it is remarkable how little notice is taken of the stars by the Vaidic poets, even the recognition of some of the luminaries as planets *i. e.* those which change their position in the heavens with regard to the fixed stars, does not appear to have occurred until considerably later.* And are not the identifications noted above too much strained and too far-fetched for taking the reason prisoner? How could the ten signs of the zodiac be said to represent the ten arms of the goddess when one of the signs (Virgo) is considered as the goddess herself, and why should the signs of the Bull, the Twin, and others be said to represent arms to which they have as little resemblance as anything with any other thing in creation. Why has the goddess three eyes, why is she said to be formed of the energy of all the gods, why did she ascend in the heavens after she came forth from Vishnu, why is she worshipped in trees and plants, why is she designated the daughter of mountain, why does she pierce the demon's heart with a lance, why does she hold the demon by the fore-lock, why is the demon encircled by a snake, why does the lion fall upon the demon and tear him up, why is she worshipped at the time of the equinoxes, why is the autumnal worship more elaborate than the vernal, why her worship, her entrance and her Visarjana are all enjoined to be performed in the morning, why is the Sandhya Puja, the puja held at the junction of two tithis regarded as the most solemn and meritorious of all others, why is she called Kaushiki, the goddess of flowers, why is the image thrown either into a fountain or a stream, why are springing grass borne on the head, why is the anointing of Durga considered so important, why is the great arati or nirajana held on the Dasami, and why is the Dasami called Vijaya, why is the

* The Taittiriya Yajurveda contains the names of the asterisms of lunar mansions, but it is well known that the work is more recent than the Rig and Sama.

goddess described as beautiful but terrific-mouthed fit to devour the universe at one gulp, why is she represented tender and powerful at the same time, why are the black goat and the buffalo sacrificed to her, and why is the festival so universally observed all over India, are questions which may strike the thinking mind, and there is but one answer for them. Because the goddess is none other than Aurora, the Dawn of the Vedas.

In the mythology of the Puranas and in the mysticisms of the Tantras this, the first and grandest of festivals so universally observed and so solemnly celebrated throughout India, was associated with a portentious event in the history of the heavens. The kingdom of heaven was in danger, the Demons and Asuras made all powerful by the suffrance of the Almighty attacked the regions of the gods, dethroned them, reduced them to the most abject condition of poverty and defied the command of the Creator himself. In this imminent crisis help was invoked of Vishnu the lord of gods. He was so indignant at beholding their wretchedness that streams of glory rushed forth from his face from which sprang Mahamaya. Streams of glory issued also from the faces of the other gods and entered the person of Mahamaya, who became a body of glory resembling a mountain on fire. The gods then gave their weapons to this lady, who in a frightful rage ascended into the air. This Pauranic myth is commemorated by the celebration of the Durgotsava, the festival of Durga, the Goddess Saviour of the gods from the scourge of the Demon. The event was of no small interest to the people of the Dark Ages of India. The Kingdom of Heaven was redeemed and the immortal gods saved from their arch enemy the Demon. Suratha a king of the Chaitra family who flourished in the Savarni (the 8th) Manvantara of the world celebrated this festival in the month of Chaitra.*

This myth of the Puranas regarding the origin of Durga, and her worship in the month of Chaitra in the spring season, under the name of Vasantotsava occurs in the Yajur Veda in a less metaphorical and more plain form. Brahma the Creator being desirous of multiplying his progeny himself became pregnant in a new form, and produced the Asuras with the thighs, and threw at them eatables in an earthen vessel. Then he destroyed the form which generated the Asuras. That form of his body became metamorphosed into dark night. He also created the gods with the mouth, and gave them nectar to drink in a golden cup, and the mouth became a bright day. The Gods are the day, and the Asuras the night. In the earlier Vedas the word Dyu, meaning day, light, is identified with the gods, and darkness, night, with the asuras.

The Dyu of the Vedas and the story of the battle between darkness and light for the kingdom of heaven have been obscured in the myth of the Puranas given above. The anecdote of Suratha (a name of the sun) the founder of the festival in the Vernal season is nothing more than an allegorical expression of the observance of the commencement of the solar year in earlier days when

*The present is the Vaivasvata (Solar) Manvantara. The Manvantara which preceded Savarni was Sarochi. A Manvantara is a cycle of four Yugas. Savarni, Sarachisa and Vaivasvata after whom the cycles are named, are all descendants of the Sun. Literally however they are different names of the sun.

the months and the asterisms coincided, and when Suratha (the sun) might be regarded as having been born in the ace of Chitra one of the asterisms in Virgo (*a* Virginis) rthe star which first appeared above the horizon on the evening of the first of Baisakha, the commencement of the year. The authors of the Sastras might have also had the idea of the junction of the sun in *a*. Virginis, with the moon in Asvini *a*. Areitis as the proper moment for commencing the year and all calculations of the Hindu calendar. The Hindus have divided the path of the sun in the heavens into twelve signs or compartments of the zodiac. These signs of the zodiac are occupied by twenty-seven asterisms or mansions of the moon, and the months of the Hindu year have been named after the mansions, in which the full moon of the solar month is supposed to take place. In the hypothetical conjunction the full moon is supposed to have happened in the lunar mansion Asvini, when the sun was in Aries. But at that time the rule of naming the month after the position of the full moon in the asterism was not known, and hence the period of the sun's stay in Aries was called by some name other than Asvina. The Vaidic names of the months (for masa or month literally means the measure of the moon and is derived from the satellite) or more accurately of the periods of the sun's stay in the twelve signs of the zodiac are Agrahyana, Taisha, Sahas, Tapasya, Madhu, Madhava, Sukra &c., and not Margasirsa, Pausha, Magha &c.

Usha the goddess Dawn, plays a most important part in the Rig Veda. "She goes to every house, she thinks of the dwelling of man, she does not despise the small or the great, she brings wealth, she is always the same immortal divine, she does not grow old, she is the young goddess, she was born of the gods to slay the powers of darkness (the Dasyus), she fills the air with light and she spreads the sky, she hides her face in water when she sees her husband. Yet she says she will come again and after the sun has travelled through the world in search of the beloved, when he is in the threshold of death, and is going to end his solitary life, she appears again in the Gloaming, the same as the Dawn, at the end of the dreary day when the sun seemed to die away in the far west, the heavens opened and the glorious image of the Dawn rose again, her beauty deepened by a gloaming darkness. O Indra thou struckest the daughter of Dyus (the Dawn) a woman difficult to vanquish".*

The above quoted passages of the Vedas are fraught with interesting meaning, and each individual sentence has been developed in the Puranas into anecdotes that fill pages.

Dawn knows no destinction of rank or wealth in her visitations. As the poet says the moon does not withhold his† light from the house of even a Chandala, so Dawn, Durga, according to the Puranas may be worshipped by men of all castes, aye even by the mlechchhas or the infidels. In her capacity of a bringer of wealth Dawn is worshipped in the form of Durga, and is prayed to bless men with plenty Dawn never grows old, nor does Durga, she is said to be full with the freshness of youth. Durga as Mahamaya was born

---

* Max Muller.

† Moon is according to the Sastras a male deity. It might be noted that the ancient authors occasionally made no distinction of sex of the gods Thus Baal is sometimes represented as a woman and Astarte bearded.

of Vishnu (the sun), and afterward she was equipped with the arms of the other gods. Indeed, the Devimahatmya which if read with the eye of a worshipper of Dawn, appears nothing more than the Pauranic abnormal development of the myth of the Dawn as fighting with the help of the gods against Darkness, night, the demon, and filling the ten quarters of the globe with her victorious sounds. In the Devimahatmya, Mahamaya is said to have been formed of the glory of Vishnu combined with those of the gods, which expressed in the language of astronomy means the twilight, formed by stray rays of many stars combined with those of the sun. Durga in the Puranas is said to be the light of fire, the light of the sun, the light of electricity, and the light of the stars, and indeed the best of all lights. The above four are indeed the sources of all light. The light generated by chemical and vital actions is the only remaining source of light, which has not been mentioned, but it needs be remembered at what age the Puranas were written, for Western Science has only so late as the eighteenth century discovered these as the only sources of light. Dawn fills the air with light, and the Puranas have expressed the same idea almost in similar words. The glory of Mahamaya filled the ten quarters of the globe. The Vaidic idea of Dawn spreading the sky has been metamorphosed in the Puranas and the Tantras into the wide and terrific-mouthed goddess, for Durga is prayed as the terrific-faced and three-eyed. Forsooth, the only distinctive peculiarity of the Dawn and the Evening is the existence of a single star in the heavens. A greater number of stars than one snakes the moment night, and the absence of any star, day.

The Dawn and the Gloaming may without violence to imagination be called terrific-mouthed,as they both. as it were swallow the universe, and the goddess Durga is ten-armed, for she embraces the universe from the ten quarters of the globe. As darkness abides in the ten quarters of the globe, Dawn challenges Darkness residing in the ten quarters all at once and with ten weapons. Dawn hides her face in water, for the rays of the sloping sun skim over the surface of water, and in the blaze of day she may be said to hide her face under it, rising once more at the gloaming time with the setting sun. The fountain and the stream are therefore considered the proper places to deposit the image of Durga, so that she may come again, for the Dawn comes again. On the death of Sati, Siva became mad, and filled with grief travelled round the world, and was about to end his solitary life wrapt in devotion for her sake, but regained his senses when Parvati married him. The Sun (Puroravas) travelled round the world and regained Dawn in her image of Gloaming at the threshold of Death. The Puranas and Tantras have developed the gloaming image of Dawn into Syama, Kali, who is also an image of Durga. The beauty of Dawn is said to have deepened in gloaming darkness, and Durga becoming Masi-coloured was metamorphosed into Kali. In the war with Mahisasura the Markandeya Purana describes Durga as the invincible lady who challenged the demon and vowed—

Whoso beateth me in battle fray,
Whoso levelleth my wonted pride,
Whoe'er my rival dares to stay,
Let him alone have me his bride.

Siva accepted the challenge, and vanquished her, and so became her husband. In the Vedas Indra is said to have struck the daughter of Dyus (the Dawn) a woman diffilcut to vanquish.

As Hari, Vishnu, is the lord of day, and is the sun, so Siva, Saumya, is the lord of night, and is the moon. Indeed, Siva bears on his forehead the crescent moon, and as such interchanges places with Vishnu the lord of day. Both are however the lord of light, and Siva being light in a milder form *i. e.* borrowed light, is the lesser deity. Siva and Hari may however be said to be identical in many respects, and as such Lakshmi and Sarasvati the twin consorts of Hari are forms of Sakti, Durga, and as Siva's is the derived light from Hari, so conversely Sarasvati and Lakshmi are regarded the daughters of Durga. Siva as lord of night has been represented in the Tantras, which view things mystically, as the most terrific of the gods, and as night is the death of day, the gods, Siva is described in the Puranas as the Destroying Energy of the Divinity. Similarly the Tantras have pursued the myth of the Gloaming as a form of Dawn, and have given numerous imaginary tales regarding the goddess Kali, a form of the Virgin, discovered by the Sun at the threshold of death, and therefore adorned with wreaths of skulls and like emblems of death. The ravens, which accompany this idol, have their counterpart in the constellation Corvus in the heavens which follows Virgo. It might be mentioned that the asterism Svati is held in the Tantras to be an auspicious junction star of the new moon for the worship of Kali.

In the Sastras Mahamaya as already observed is said to have come forth in the form of glory from the person of Vishnu and to have ascended the heavens, figuring like a mountain on fire. The explanation of this myth is that the rays of the morning sun kiss the mountain tops and tinge them red, giving them the appearance of a body on fire, and that light of the sun descends below from the top of the mountain, the Dawn has been described by the Puranas as the descendant or daughter of Himavat, the prominent range of mountains in the north. Dawn discovers the trees and their fruits by her light, and Durga is therefore worshipped in trees. Trees and plants are the abode of Durga, for Dawn peeps through the windows of their foliage. As Dawn with her solitary ray of light passing through the crevices of the caves pierces as it were the heart of demon Darkness, and sucks out its blood in the redness imparted to the sky by the rising sun, so Durga plunges a spear into the breast of the Asura and draws forth blood from it. Dawn, Durga, predominates and holding the demon Darkness, encircled by eternity (the snake emblem of eternity) by the forelock subdues him by planting her foot on his shoulder. Durga stands with one foot on a lion whose Sanskrit name is Hari, the god of day, the sun, and the other on the demon Darkness, for Dawn may be said to stand on both. The left foot of Durga, with which she crushes the demon, is raised a little in the attitude of employing force, for Dawn virtually makes the demon Darkness bear her weight. As the sun, upon which Dawn may be said to ride, chases away darkness into shadows, so the lion of Durga tars the Asura into pieces.

The Dakshinayana is the night of the gods and the Uttarayana their day. The equinoxes, therefore, are the Dawn and the Gloaming of the gods, the proper moments for worshipping Durga, the Dawn of the Puranas. The Morning of the Equinoxes is the Dawn of Dawns, and hence held sacred to the worship of Durga the goddess Dawn. From the text and the notes it will be seen that the Sastras have laid great stress upon the performance in morning of all ceremonies connected with the worship of Durga, Dawn. According to the Puranas the term Sandhya, junction,Twilight, includes both the Dawn and the Gloaming, but the Tantras have extolled the Gloaming, evening, *the* Sandhya par *excellence,* and the worship of Sandhya therefore has superseded that of Dawn. The principal puja of Durga is accordingly held at the great Sandhya of Ashtami and Navami Tithis, a moment very near the centre of the bright fortnight. From the Navami tithi of the bright fortnight the reign of Light may be said to prevail. Springing grass is the emblem of light, for the sun brings forth the plants and the corn, and in the worship of Dawn the precursor of Light, the sun, springing grass is borne on head as the token of the festival. With the approach of spring, which follows the Vernal Equinox plants revive and blossoms burst forth in profuseness and Dawn is therefore said to have appeared in the form of blossoms.

Both the diurnal and the hexamensic Dawns are considered auspicious moments for bathing, and the anointing of Durga at that time is for the same reason held to be meritorious.

Dawn having vanquished the demon Darkness establishes the reign of Light. Durga is therefore designated Vijaya, Victoria, or the bestower of victories. It is remarkable that the constellation of Berenice is on the north of Virgo.

The dark fortnight of a lunar month is the period, when darkness predominates and is therefore considered unfit for certain ceremonies. In the bright fortnight also for seven or eight days there is a contest as it were between Darkness and Light, and it is only on the dasami tithi, the tenth lunation, that the dominion of light is thoroughly established. Following this natural phenomenon in the worship of Durga, the Dasami (Vijaya) may be regarded as the celebration of the victory of Dawn over Darkness, and as the martial exploits of the ancients were commemorated by the presentation or lustration of arms in review so the triumph of Dawn over Darkness is similarly celebrated by the presentation or lustration of (lights) the weapons of Dawn.

Black kid is the most acceptable sacrifice to Durga, Dawn, for blacknight is her victim, and for the same reason the Sastras enjoin that in the Vasanti Puja, dark flowers should be offered to Durga. In sacrificing a goat to Durga the animal is directed to be fixed between cloud-formed pillars and between the pillars which divide the universe.* At the approach of Dawn, Darkness is fixed between hazy clouds or properly speaking between the zones of condensed vapour hovering over the horizon, and made palpable in the east and west by the rising and setting sun. Night, Darkness, the demon is fixed between the pillars of Dawn and Gloaming, which divide the day of twenty-four hours or of the Equinoxes which divide the starry heaven into two.

Durga is gold coloured for Dawn is red as gold. But the Bengal pratima has other figures than Durga. Ganesa (Janus) is the God of morning and of day after whom the

---

* The Sloka in the text has been translated otherwise. The Sanscrit is 'Meghakara stambha."

first month of the year Januarius has been named by the Romans. He is called Ganapati by the Hindus and is the first of a group of gods. He is red coloured as the Brahma Murti of the rising sun. He sits on a lotus, which opens at the approach of the sun. Lakshmi is the ten o'clock sun and she therefore stands on a lotus. Sarasvati is the two o'clock sun the hottest and the brightest and therefore the whitest sun of the day. Kartikeya is the setting sun and is painted yellow. According to certain interpretations of the Puranas and Tantras, Durga has been made to assume a different character, that is Force, Prakrti, Sakti. But when it is remembered that man's idea of the godhead in the infancy of the world was derived from the manifestations of the sun, moon and stars, the identification of Durga with Dawn, it is to be hoped, will not appear altogether extravagant. Indeed, this theory finds a remarkable confirmation in the Invokation to the Goddess sung by Kalidasa in his Sakuntala or the Lost Ring quoted in the title-page. This sublime sloka, though rendered differently by different translators, literally means as follows :

"That which is the first work of the Creator (Light of Dawn), that which bears away the Ghi offered according to law (Light of Fire), that which is sacrificer himself (Light of Life), those two which regulate time (the Dawn and the Gloaming), that which pervades the universe possessed with the object of hearing* (Space), that which is said to be the energy of all growth (Light of the Sun), and that with which the animate are living : May Isa, Great God, apparent in these eight benign forms bless you ! Amen !"

* Rendered literally this passage means that which pervades the universe being qualified as Usha the object (of worship) of Sruti (the Vedas.)

DURGA PUJA.

[*The following paper was originally published in the "Hindoo Patriot" for the 23rd October,* 1871.]

THE PRATIMA OR THE GROUP OF FIGURES(1).—CONST RUCTION.

On the day of Ratha Yatra, *i. e.* on the second day of the bright half of the month of Ashadha, a piece of bamboo-slit of the required length is properly cleaned and smoothed and rounded by the kumbhakara (potter,) and then taken up to the room where the family idols are kept; the family priest, after worshipping Vishnu, anoints it with chandan, a sandal-wood paste, and invokes Durga upon it. This piece of bamboo-slit remains in the same room till on the eighth day of the waning moon of Sravana, *i. e.* till the Janmashtami, when the architect of the pratima brings it down. The frame-work (katamo) is then commenced. The materials are scrupulously collected, and every precaution is taken to preserve their purity (*i. e.* freedom from defilement by unbelievers.) The materials are pieces of bambco-slits, unpealed garan (Ceriops

Roxburghianus, Arn) yearlings, dried ulu grass, (Imperata cylindrica, Beauv) and a plank from mango timber. The carpenter then drills holes in the plank at an auspicious moment, and the kumar builds the framework upon it. Rough skeletons of the idols are made with ulu straw, and then a dough of earth from the Hugli, cow-dung, and husk of rice is made up, and with the earth thus prepared the kumar moulds up the figures. These are seven in number, four of which are removeable, and the principal three, which are centrical in the group, are attached to one another. All the figures, except one of the lower-most figures of the central group and the right-most one, are first made headless. The heads are prepared by the kumar at his house. The figures are then allowed to dry for about a fortnight or twenty days, when again an auspicious moment is fixed upon for covering over the idols with a plaster of finer earth, and it is then that the heads to those figures, which had not been fixed unto them, and the fingers of all the figures, are put on. The snake, which encircles one of the centrical figures, is at this time formed, so also the top-piece or chal as it is called. The small nooks on both sides of the frame-work are next fitted up with two groups of figures, and miniature weapons and the head of a buffalo, and a mouse are then moulded. Indeed, before the waning fortnight of Asvina the kumar finishes his work and then the figures are left to dry for some days. The painter enters appearance generally on the third or the fourth day of the waning fortnight of Asvina and paints figures according to the directions given in the Sastras. On the fourth or rather the third day of the waning fortnight of Asvina *i. e.*, about three or four days before the puja the mali(2) decorates the idols with tinsel and imitation ornaments. The idols are ready for worship on the evening of the sixth day of the waxing fortnight of Asvina. On the plank of wood is raised about a foot high a platform of wicker-work covered with plaster of earth. On this platform rest all the figures, their real weight being supported by horizontal props attached to the strong frame-work of bamboo-slits and garan, which is shaded from the front view partly by the figures themselves and partly by plaster of earth. Supported on the frame-work of the back is the richly moulded chal, divided into three semi-circular compartments, with the convex sides projecting upwards. In each compartment are painted, according to the injunctions of the Sastras, figures of various gods and goddesses, and scenes of several battle-fields. From the two upper-most corners of the frame-work project two figures of Nilakantha bird, Coraccias indicas.

Peculiar customs are observed by some families in the construction of the idols. In families where the Durgotsava is an ancient institution, the idols are constructed wholly either by men of the carpenter caste or by men of the potter caste. These hold chakran lands granted to them, or rather to their ancestors, and the only return they make is the service rendered in the construction of the idols. The carpenter or the potter comes on the prescribed day of every year and prepares the pratima without any reference to the head of the house. In this manner others, who likewise hold rent-free lands, from the priest who performs the worship to the suppliers of different edibles including the musicians and other attendants on the occasion, render their annual tribute of service, and the festival is celebrated without subjecting the family to additional expenses. At places where the ulu straw is not available the substratum of the figures is made with the straw of paddy. In some families however the same frame-work is used every year, and when the plank gets rotten, a bit from the old plank is attached to the new. The tenth day of the waxing fortnight of Ashadha is in some families observed as the day sacred to the construction of the idol. In others, again, the Janmashtami or the birth day of Krshna is preferred. No respectable family, however, purchases a ready-made idol from the bazar. The chal or the canvas top of the frame-work varies in form in different families. Some have a round chal, which is in Bengali called Bangala, others have three separate semi-circular, triangular, spherically-triangular pieces, with truncated conical top.

The figures are, in the central group, a representation of Durga, the ten-armed goddess, standing with the right foot upon the back of a lion, which is again described in the attitude of a combatant attacking an Asura, (the buffalo-demon) on whom rests her left foot. The goddess has many-braided locks of hair, the crescent moon on her forehead; three eyes, and a face, resembling in brightness the full moon, her complexion as brilliant as liquid gold; her stature gracefully thrice-bent; and her eyes exquisitely beautiful. With the freshness of youth, and completely decorated with ornaments; with a lovely set of teeth, and with bosoms lofty and compact, the goddess is represented in the attitude of destroying the buffalo-demon, with ten arms delicate and rounded as the tender stalks of the lotus, holding the trident in one of her right arms, the sword and the discus in the lower ones, a sharp dart and a lance in the other two respectively ; while in her left arms holding the shield, the bent bow, the noose, the goad and the bell or the axe. The buffalo is represented as a headless trunk, from which springs up a demon, with a shield and sword in hand, pierced in his breast by the lance of the goddess and besmeared with blood, gushing from his wounds. The goddess frowning with a terrifies contraction of her brows, holds in her left hand with the forelocks of the demon the serpent noose, which strangles the Asura in its dreadful coil, while the lion falls upon him, with teeth gorging blood. The right foot of the goddess rests lightly on the back of the lion, while she stands tip-toe, with her left foot on the demon's shoulder.

The figure to the right of the group of three(3), is that of Lakshmi. She is represented as standing on a full-blown white lotus, with her right foot slightly bent over the left, with the toe of the right a little turned out. The whole figure slightly leans towards the right and in her each hand, she holds a full-blown white lotus. In the Sastras, she is described as bright as gold, decorated with necklaces, yellowish gold and silvery white, standing on a lotus, her right hand raised and the left lowered, making a graceful attitude. To the left of the central group is put Sarasvati as white as marble or purer still, like the jasmine, the moon, or the snow, standing on a white lotus and holding in her hands a vina, guitar, dressed in white. Her left foot rests tip-toe on the right and her left hand slightly raised. She leans gracefully towards the left. A little lower to the right of Lakshmi sits, with his left leg bent on the right the vermeil-red, triple-eyed, plump and round-bodied, big-bellied, handsome Ganesa, holding in his hands a lotus flower, a noose, a goad, and chakra ; surmounted by the face of the prince of elephants, one-tusked bearing the crescent moon on his forehead, from the pores of which distill liquor drops. His shoulders are decorated with a wreath made of the king of serpents and his dress is red. To the left of Sarasvati sits the victorious and gold-colored Kartikeya, on a beautiful peacock. In his right hand, he holds a lance and with the open left palm confers boons on his devotees. Under the lotus, the seat of Ganesa, may be seen a small crouching mouse, snugly resting with its tail curved on its back.

In the right nook of the frame-work is placed Siva, seated on his fat Nandi(bull). Siva is described as having two arms and one head, three dull, half-shut eyes, a crescent and a head-dress of serpents. He holds in his right hand a damaru, a small drum instrument, resembling two inverted cones. It is sounded by the oscillation of a small knot hanging from a string and striking alternately the drums on the two sides. In his left hand Siva holds on high his enormous horn. In the left nook sits Ramachandra, green colored, on his favourite monkey, Hanuman. He holds in each hand an arrow and a bow.

On the lower platform are placed two small figures of two girl attendants, Jaya and Vijaya, the one is painted yellow and the other red; under the Asura is seen a small representation of a severed head of a buffalo.

The chals(4) constitute the most interesting part of the entire group. The principal and prominent picture in the central chal, is that of Muktakesi, a form of Kali. She is painted purple and in every respect she is a Kali. Her red tongue projecting out of her purple though well-formed face, four-armed, decorated with a necklace of human skulls and dressed in elephant-skin. She also stands upon Siva, but unlike the Dakshina Kali her left leg is foremost. Above the figure of Kali are painted the pictures of the avatars, the first four of which,

Matsya, Kachchha, Varaha, and Nrsinha, are towards the right. Buddha is placed in the centre and he is represented seated in deep meditation with his eyes closed and both hands folded on the navel. Towards the left are Vamana, Parasurama, Valarama and Kalki. Rama, the complement of the ten avatars, is the principal figure of the chal towards the right. Round Muktakesi are placed the ten Mahavidyas *i. e.*, the ten incarnations of Sakti viz. Kali, the well known goddess. Tara, another form of Kali, represented as more plump than Kali, with legs differently disposed, that is stretching side-ways. Dhumavati, Shodasi, Bhuvanesvari and Vagala are milder incarnations of Sakti. They are all represented as seated, some upon chairs held by Brahma, Vishnu, Siva and Narada, some as being anointed with waters poured by elephants. Chhinnamastaka is a redish brown, naked, headless goddess, she stands upon a human couple and in one hand holds a gory scimitar and in the other, her own severed head, which drinks the warm blood, gushing forth from her headless trunk. Matangi, Bhairavi and Siddhavidya have each a place in the chal.

In the lower compartment of this central chal are represented the several elementary gods, viz.,

Indra the god of the firmament, Agni the god of fire, Varuna the god of waters, the Maruts the god of the winds and Yama the god of death and the eight Saktis viz. Ugrachanda, Prachanda, Chandogra, Chandanayica, Chanda, Chandavati, Chandarupa, and Atichandica, and below these, in a small compartment, is represented the battle between the gods and the demons.

The principal group in the right chal is that of Ramachandra, seated on a throne with Sita at his left, his favourite monkey Hanuman kneeling, and his three brothers Bharata, Lakshmana and Satrughna holding an umbrella and fans respectively. In this chal is also represented the battle of Rama and Ravana. The sun is seated in his car drawn by seven horses, and the tainted moon has also a place in this compartment. On the top is represented Siva, in his marriage dress ; and small figures of the sixty Yoginis are given. In the lower compartment is delineated the scene of the battle of Sumbha and Nisumbha, and the principal figure in this group, is that of the gold-colored goddess, the two-armed Chandi, with a lance in hand resting on a lion.

In the left chal the principal figure is that of Radha, seated on a throne, with her Gopinis all round, dressed as a queen, and Krshna doing homage to her. In this chal is also represented the battle of the Kurus and Pandavas, and in the lower compartment is described another scene of the battle of the demons with the black form of Sakti. She is represented as a two-armed goddess, standing on a lion and holding swords in both hands. In the several smaller corners are represented the Vatukas and the nine Grahas (planets) viz., the Sun, the Moon, the Mars the Venus, the Jupiter, the Mercury, the Saturn, the Rahu and the Ketu (the ascending and the descending nodes.)

In some families the paintings of the chals differ greatly, and some of the above-mentioned gods and goddesses are left out, according to the forms and dimensions of the *chal*. The painter, however, takes great care to so dispose the several figures, that the effect of the entire collection is rendered graceful and imposing. Certain modifications are observed in coloring the several idols and in the disposition of the same. Ganesa is generally painted red, all over the body, except the trunk which is that of a white elephant ; the Malliks of Andul have a two-armed Ganesa ; some however have light orange or light green Ganesa in some families, again, he is represented as standing. No variations occur in the coloring of

Lakshmi, Sarasvati and Durga, though some have the first two transposed and the last with four arms only. Some have what is called, an Abhaya murti *i. e.* a two-armed Durga seated with Siva. The Buffalo-demon is represented by some as coming out of the carcass of a buffalo and is somewhere painted gray. Kartikeya is always represented as seated on a peacock. Sometimes we meet with a standing Kartikeya and then he is painted yellowish white. In some families the clothes of the three female idols are made by the architect with plasters of earth, and in others, pieces of cloth are actually placed round the idols, and in the latter case the color preferred for the golden colored female idols is red and for pure white Sarasvati blue or purple. In some families, again, the principal ornaments of the idols are made of earth. But Kartikeya is most susceptible of change. His dress depends much upon the fancy of the head of the family. The heads of Kartikeya, Ganesa and the demon are the same in every house. The heads of the three goddesses may be either slightly flat or oval. Many have an elongated head for the lion, more like that of a horse and a dragon, while others, delineate the natural face of the lion.

With these gods and goddesses, some of which are represented in clay and others in paint, is worshipped perhaps, with equal respect the Navapatrica or the group of nine plants or twigs of plants. The Mallikas of Andul establish two Navapatricas, the one on the dark navami and the other on the evening preceding the Saptami. In the minor details both in construction of the idols and in the worship there are so many variations and peculiar customs observed in different families, that it is difficult to lay down any practice as universal, except the universal celebration of the Autumnal Festival. The Chaudhuris of Makardah, for example, do not offer any eatables to the goddess on the occasion of the festival during the day. At night boiled rice is offered in dishes made of plantain leaves. (5)

PAINTING THE IDOLS.

As soon as the idols are dry, the painter comes in and lays on the figures three or four coatings of a water-paint made of chalk. This forms the ground, and when it gets sufficiently dry, Durga, Lakshmi and Kartikeya are painted yellow with harital, sulphurate of arsenic, which is ground and mixed carefully with water and gum from the Vel fruit. Ganesa is painted similarly with hingul, a coarse ore of sulphuret of mercury, and the demon with jangal, verdigris, done up with a varnish of garjan oil(6). And all these figures are subsequently covered with a varnish. The Lion and Sarasvati are painted with another preparation of chalk, and are polished by the surface being rubbed with fine linen. The painter forgets not to put on the forehead and arms of the goddesses the usual tatoo marks.

As soon as the painting of the idols is finished, the remnants of the paint are taken to the ladies of the house, and they paint with the same a particular spot in the room alloted to the family idol. After the paints are sufficiently dry, at an auspicious moment the entire group is removed to the place of worship, and is set up on a raised platform of wood, which is washed and painted over by the ladies of the house with a white paint made of ground rice, the designs on the platform being a bed of lotuses, the feet of the goddesses, and a series of yantras, mystic figures(7). This platform or low table, about 1½ feet high, is placed upon clay, and beneath it are sprinkled the five grains, rice, wheat, barley, mas (Phaseolus Roxburghii, Wight) and sesamum. In about three or four days small seed lings of a whitish yellow color spring up beneath the table.

THE WORSHIP.

In the autumn of every year is to be celebrated the Mahapuja, is the injunction of the

Markandeya Purana. It is not optional, it is indeed a commandment, and it has what the Smarthas would call a Nityatva *i. e.*, the omission is a sin, but it has also a Kamyatva in it, *i. e.*, if performed it is meritorious and may be performed with some object in view. The Kalika Purana says, whoever in the great festival of Durga does not worship the Devi whether from ignorance, vanity, or jealousy, or from any other cause, the wrath of the Goddess falls on him and destroys all his wishes. The Bhavishyottara Purana says, the gratification of Bhavani is the assurance of happiness for the whole year, is for the destruction of the spirits, goblins and ghosts, and also for the sake of festivity. The Devi Purana says, the meritorious effects of gratifying Durga even for half a minute, cannot be described by Mahesa, the five-faced, in a hundred years. Indeed, the Durgotsava is of all Hindu festivals, the most solemn and the most popular. Every Hindu, who can afford to enjoy the luxury of celebrating the festival, begins to make preparations for it from the commencement of the year. So dear is the festival to the Hindus of Bengal that few forego the pleasure of worshipping the autumnal Goddess. Should not the circumstances of any person permit him to worship the Goddess in the idols, in his own house, he worships her in paintings or in the Ghata (an earthen pot of a peculiar form), or he sends his free-will and devotional offerings to the idols of his neighbours or relatives. On the eighth day of the moon *i. e.* on the second day of the Durgotsava offerings of rice, sugar, cocoanut, and various other fruits and flowers are made by every Hindu in Bengal. The Devi Purana says, this is a ceremony that can be celebrated by Brahmanas, Kshatrias, Vaisyas, Sudras, and by other slaves, also by various Mlechchhas, and Dasyus. Indeed, it is a national festival, and no native of any caste or creed can avoid the contagion of the jubilee. In the North-West, in the Punjab and in the Southern Presidency it is observed as a Navaratri (nine nights) festival.

The festival is celebrated according to the text of three Puranas viz., the Kalika Purana, the Devi Purana, and the Vrhannandikesvara Purana; the most elaborate of these is the last. There are three times of commencing the ceremony. From the waning ekadasi of Ashadha to the waxing ekadasi of Kartika the gods are said to sleep, this period is called the Dakshinayana, the night of the Gods, when the sun proceeds towards the south. Before the goddess is worshipped she has to be awakened. Indra is said to rise about the time of the new moon of Asvina, and from time immemorial the Sakrotthana or the rising of Indra has been observed as an agricultural festival. The Devi Purana says, in the month of Isha *i.e.* Asvina, in the waning fortnight, when the sun enters the sign Virgo, on the ninth day, the Goddess is to be roused with sport, pleasure, and prosperity. On the sixth day, with the asterism Jyaishtha (R and T, Scorpionis) the Vel tree is to be invited; on the seventh, with the asterism Mula, the entrance of the patricas is to be celebrated; on the eighth day, with Purvashadha asterism are to be performed with fast the puja and the homas; on the ninth day, with the asterism Uttarashadha, Siva is to be worshipped with balis; and on the tenth day, with the asterism Sravana the goddess being homaged is to be consigned to water. In the Kamakhya Panchamurti Prakrana, it is stated, that as long as there are the earth, the air, the heavens, water, fire, the moon, and the planets, so long shall the worship of Chandica be observed on the earth, for in ancient days on the eighth and ninth days of Asvina used to be celebrated with great eclat, the autumnal festival. It is added that in ancient times on the ninth day in autumn the goddess used to be awakened, the ceremony has accordingly been known as the great Autumnal Festival. The Linga Purana says, after worship, on the ninth day of the dark fortnight of Asvina the Devi is to be awakened with great pomp and eclat. This is called the Bodhana or the arousing. The Bodhana may also be commenced on the sixth day of the waxing moon of Asvina. The Bhavishya Purana says, on the sixth the goddess is to be aroused in the Vel tree, and the evening prayer offered with devotion. The Kalika Purana says, on the sixth, the Devi is to be awakened on a branch of the Vel tree and on a pair of its fruits, on the seventh, the same being collected She is to be worshipped thereon; on the eighth, on the same twig She is to be worshipped with some peculiar ceremonies, and the worshipper is to watch the whole night with vigilance, and in the dead of night to offer a sacrifice; on the ninth, with numerous sacrifices She is to be worshipped and to be meditated with the Durga mantra; and on the tenth the idol is to be consigned to water, and the jubilee conclud-ed with the time-honored custom of kolakuli or embracing. From the above it would appear, that the commencement of the ceremony of arousing the goddess may be deserved on either the ninth day of the dark fortnight preceding the Durgotsava, or on the sixth day of the waxing fort-night. These two are the days of Bodhana or arousing, but the Kalpa or the resolution to worship the Goddess may be commenced on the first day after the new moon preceding the Durgotsava, this is called the Pratipadadikalpa.

THE KALPARAMBHA(8).

SANKALPA.—On the day of pratipada having finished the usual morning ceremony, (9) with kusa in hand, and having done the achamana(10), repeat the achamana sukta. The achamana is a peculiar process of washing and purifying one's self. The head of the family then says, Om the gods always observe that Vishnu is the best of all existences, and He indeed is the eye of knowledge &c. He then worships Narayana, and utters, Om Svasti, Prosperity. Om in this performable yearly autumnal great Durga Puja oh ye (addressing the priests present) pronouncee that ye are pure. I am pure is the reply. Similarly Svasti and Rddhi are repeated, and the Svasti Sukta is pronounced. Om may Indra, the lord of sacrifices, bless us with prosperity, may Pusha the Visvaveda bless us with prosperity, and may Vrhaspati bless us with prosperity! Om the sun, the moon, Yama, time, evening, beings, day, night, air, the dikpalas (gods presiding over the points of the compass) the earth, the heavens, the aerial beings and the immortals, witnesses appointed by Brahma, may they descend on this spot(11). Having repeated the above and placed in the udumvara (12) filled with water a nutmeg, a flower, a few blades of kusa grass, a leaf of tulsi and sesamum, the head of the family, with his face towards the north, holds the kosa in his both hands and kneeling repeats, Vishnur Om tat sat and utters the following, "commencing from to-day in the month of Asvina, waxing fortnight, Pratipada tithi, to the Navami (9th) tithi, every day I so and so of such and such gotra with a view to propitiate Sri Durga, do hereby promise, after the usual worshipping of Ganesa and other gods to perform the yearly autumnal worship of Sribhagavat Durga, according to the Vrhannandikesvara Purana." The yajamana then drops the sacred water towards the north-east corner. While he thus drops water the officiating priests, one and all, repeat the sankalpa sutras(13). Similarly a sankalpa is made for reading the DEVI MAHATMYA from the Markandeya Purana as follows:

Vishnur Om tat sat, commencing from to-day, month of Asvina, waxing fortnight, pratipada tithi to the Navami, I, so and so, of such and such gotra, in the performance of the yearly autumnal Durga worship, do hereby promise to read that portion of the Jayakhya Markandeya Purana, which commences with "Markandeya said 'Savarni surya tanayo' &c." and ends with "Savarni bhavita manu" so many times every day.

VARANA.—Then comes the Varana or appointment of the officiating priests. The yajamana, to sit with his face towards the east and the priests facing north. The yajamana says, Om you are sadhu, the priests reply, Om we are sadhu and we are seated. The yajamana says, Om I wish to propitiate you; the priests reply, Om do so. Then the yajamana anoints the priests with chandan and offers them flowers, clothes, ornaments, &c., and holding their right knee repeats, Vishnur om tat sat, to-day in the month of Asvina and in the Pratipada tithi of the bright fortnight I, so and so, of such and such gotra, do hereby appoint you who are duly homaged with chandan &c., so and so, of such and such gotra, to perform my promised annual autumnal Durga Puja. The priest replies, om I am appointed, and then the yajamana says, do you perform the same according to the Sastras, to which the priest rejoins, I shall perform the same according to my knowledge. Similarly the Tantradharakar, (14) the hota, the reader of the Devimahatmya and other officiating priests are appointed. As soon as all the officiating priests are so appointed, the yajamana is set free. The priests then commence the usual worship.

GHATASTHAPANA(15) :—A ghata is a large earthen water jar ; it should not be less than half a cubit in height and not larger than two cubits. It has a ring at the bottom, so that it may be safely placed on earth without being capsized. Its form is peculiar ; the central portion buldges out prominently, and the collar is extraordinarily narrow, the brim is broad and open, and indeed turns out like a bell-shaped flower. Such a ghata is filled with Ganga water, and a twig of mango, a twig of Asvattha (religious fig), one of Bata (Indian fig,) one of Asoka (jonesia) and one of jack fruit are put in it, two betel-leaves with stalk are placed upon it, also a shallow earthen dish filled with rice : upon the rice rests a cocoanut husk and stalk all, with the long stiff stalk facing the priests. A piece of new cloth dyed yellow with turmeric is tied round the neck of the ghata, and a figure of a God with two arms and two legs is described on the central portion of the ghata, with a paste made of vermillion and ghee. The ghata thus decorated is placed upon a lump of fine dough of clay, brought from the River, over which are scattered the five grains. In a small earthen pot a mixture of curd and rice is made, which is sprinkled on the ghata. Every process above described is performed by the priest with a separate mantra. When the ghata is filled with water the priest invokes all the river gods on the ghata, and then reads a Sukta from the Vedas, which means. Om you are the offspring of Varuna, om you are the dominion of Varuna, om you are the companion of Varuna, om Varuna is your associate, om Varuna do you approach. The clay is placed with the following incantation : Om you are Bhu, om you are Bhumi, om you are Aditi, om you are the supporter of the universe,om you are the material of this world, om you are the earth, om you are home, om do you not destroy this world. Then taking a handful of unhusked rice the priest repeats the following, and scatters the same on the dough : Om you are rice, om you are life, you are the life of the gods, you are our life, you are our internal life, you are long life, you give life, om the Sun with his rays gives you the milk of life and Varuna nourishes you with water. Similarly the other grains are scattered, and the ghata is then placed upon them with the following mantra. Om noble-souled jar, you please the gods, you held in your cavity the sacred nectar, from you oozed out a thousand drops of liquor, which made the gods immortal, om you saved the gods, may you save' me. The twigs are placed in the ghata with the following mantra, Om the producers, the desert is suchwithout you, life is death without you, the sun is unbearable without you. How he scorches with his burning rays, you save even your enemies the wood-cutters from the sun, you are most noble, and you rule over every region. The cocoanut is placed with the following mantra. Om whatever bears fruits, whatever bears not, whatever bears blossoms, whatever is flowerless, they are all the offsprings of Vrhaspati, may they purify me and this house. Then taking the vermillion paste on the fourth finger, Om like the Ocean you are vast, Indra loves you, with ghee when dropped you describe a continuous stain. You are noble, perhaps nobler than the fuel-wood, which paints everything black. The priest then holds a lotus flower in his hand and repeating the following, places it on the ghata, Om you are sri, you are beautiful, you are Lakshmi's self by day, and by night, you are the stars as beautiful as the Asvina, you are desired by us, loved by many, loved by all. The ghata is then placed carefully and made steady with the following mantra, Om thick-bellied, thin collared, be you soon steady, steady against the winds, against the earths motion, be you are earth, you are well-formed, you are made of earth. Om commencing from Ganga all the rivers, all the seas, all the oceans, all tanks, lakes, &c., come and destroy the evils of the yajamana.

THE PRELIMINARY PUJAS.

CERTAIN ceremonies are observed before every puja, and these are the arghyasthapana, the establishing of the ordinary oblation; the asana suddhi or the purifying of the carpet, on which the priest sits; the bhutasuddhi, or the purifying of the elements of which the body is composed; the dhyana or the meditation of the image of the god to be worshipped; the Nyases, and the worship of the several minor gods.

Before the establishment of the ordinary arghya, a handful of white mustard is taken, and it is scattered all about with the following mantra,(16) Om may those beings, who live on this earth, and who throw obstacles to the worship, the unbelievers and infidels, be removed and destroyed by command of Siva. Om vetalas, pisachas, rakshas, and all reptiles, may they be removed, for I am worshipping Durga. Then a bali is made of mas and curd, and with a handful of the same, the following mantra is repeated; Om bhutas, pretas, pisachas and others, whoever dwell here, may they receive this bali distributed by me. With a flower the following mantra is uttered :—May they, who have been propitiated by bali, and worshipped with flowers, withdraw from this place, and let me worship Durga. Om phat to the weapons. Then taking fried rice, chandan, mustard, fruits, flowers, rice, and durva(17) seven times repeat Om phat to the weapons. Scatter the same all round with the following mantra, Om may those beings, who are the protectors of this earth be removed that I may worship Durga in their absence.

THE ARGHYASTHAPANA(18).—The shastras enjoin the following directions to the priest for the formation of the arghya : Describe a triangle on the left and worship it with a flower uttering these words, Om obeisance to the Sust aining Force Upon it place the tripod, and after washing the conchshell with Om phat, and putting it on the tripod, fill three-four this of it with water, repeating the mantra Om nama. Put rice and durva on the conchshell, and with the following mantra and goad-mudra invoke the descent of the several holy rivers from the solar sphere, Om Ganga, Yamuna, Godavari, Sarasvati, Narmada, Sindhu Caveri, come into this water, and then worship them. Place chandan and flower with Om in the water, present the dhenumudra, and with Hum cover the two fore-fingers, and ten times repeat the mulamantra, and taking some water from the conchshell sprinkle it on the offerings with the words, Om Phat; and let the priest purify himself with the same. Put a flower on the opening of the conchshell and worship the janitor gods, Om obeisance, Om this flower and chandan to the janitor gods. Then repeat the following: Om obeisance to Vastupurusha and to Brahma in the south-west corner. Clap thrice over the head, and with phat strike the earth with the left foot.

THE ASANASUDDHI.—Holding the carpet repeat, Om the rshi of asana mantra is Meruprshtha, its metre is sutala, its deity is tortoise, it is used in sitting on carpets. Om you hold the world and the earth, and you are held by Vishnu. Do you hold me always and do you purify this carpet. And holding a flower Om hrim this flower to the Sustaining Force, the lotus-seated goddess(19).

THE BHUTA SUDDHI(23).—It is a peculiar mystical tantric rite. Holding a scented flower anointed with chandan on the left temple repeat, Om obeisance to the teachers; on the right, Om to Ganesa; on the cheeks, Om to Durga. Then with Om phat rub the palms with flowers, and clap thrice over the head, and by snapping the fingers at ten different directions secure immunity from them.

Next utter the mantra Ram, sprinkle water all around, and suppose this water as a wall of fire. Place the hands on the lap with palms upwards. Let the priest in imagination identify himself with the animal spirit (jivat-ma) abiding in man's breast in the form of the tapering flame of a lamp, unite it with (Kulakundalini) the material Goddess, seated in (muladhara) the stamina of the body (the Coccyx ?) and conduct it by means of the Susamna nerve through the six spheres within the body named, Manipura, Svadhisthana, Muladhara, Anahata, Visuddha, and Ajnana, upwards to the Divine Spirit, residing in the pericarp of a thousand-petalled lotus, bent downwards from the cranium, and join them together. Then meditate the 24 essences in nature as concentrated in the amalgam, viz., the five cardinal elements, earth, water, fire, air, and space, the five external organs of sense the nose, the tongue, the eyes, the skin and the ears, with their objects, *i. e.* scent,taste, form, touch, and sound, the five organs of action viz. the mouth, the feet and hands, the pudendum, and the organ, and all forms, whether material, mental, or intellectual, with those of self-consciousness, self-cogitation, or egoism.

Conceive in the left nostril, the mantra Yam which is described as fume-colored, and declared to be the vija or root of wind, repeat it 16 times while drawing air by the same nostril, then close the nose and hold the breath which is inherent in man, by assuming the kumbhaka form, and repeat 64 times the mantra. Purify the body by washing with Yam the black male form of Sin seated in the left cavity of the thorax, and let out the breath through the right nostril, while repeating the mantra 32 times.

Conceive in the right nostril the red mantra Ram, the root of fire, and fill the body with air, while repeating the mantra sixteen times. Purify the body by burning the male form of sin with the fire arising from the lower parts of the body. Then close the nose and hold the breath, while repeating sixty-four times the mantra. Exhale the ashes with the breath through the left nostril accompanied with 32 recitals of the mantra.

Similarly the white mantra Tham, the root of the moon, is to be established with the moon on the forehead, and the wind to be inhaled, retained and exhaled as stated before with 64 recitations of Vam, the root of Varuna. Then from the moon in the forehead is to be extracted the nectar as the essence of the progenitrix, and the entire body to be thus formed with 32 recitations Lam, the root of earth, strengthening the so generated body, exhale air through the right nostril.

THE EXTERNAL MATRIKA NYASA.—The rshi of this Matrika mantra is Brahma, its metre is Gayatri, the deity Matrika sarasvati, the consonants are the roots, the vowels are the Saktis, these are used in the Matrika Nyasa. With a flower Om obeisance to Brahma Rshi in the head, Om obeisance to Gayatri Metre in the mouth, Om to Matrika Sarasvati Devi in the heart, Om to the consonant roots in the muladhara, Om to the vowel Saktis in the feet. Then meditate on Matrika :(21) Help me O ! goddess of speech, whose lips are parted by fifty characters, whose arms extend to the knees, whose bosom is well formed, whose forehead is emblazoned by the moon with all the phases, whose breasts are as compact as they are lofty, and whose hands hold the mudra, the beadstring, a nectar-pot, and gift of knowledge, and who is white in appearance, and three-eyed.

Am to the forehead, Am to the mouth, Im to the right eye, Im to the left eye, Um to the right ear, Um to the left ear, Rm to the right nose, Rm to the left nose, Im to the right cheek, Im to the left cheek, Em to the upper lip, Aim to the lower lip, Om to the upper teeth, Aum to the lower teeth, Am to the cerebrum, Ah to the right shoulder-blade, Kam to the elbow, Kham to the wrist, Gam to the roots of the phalanges, Gham to the phalanges, Nam to the nails, Cham to the left shoulder-blade, Chham to the left elbow, Jam to the left wrist, Jham to the roots of the left phalanges, Nam to the left nails. Tam to the right heels, Tham to the right knee-bone, Dam to the right ankle, Dham to the roots of the phalanges, Lam to the tarsals. Similarly Tam, Tham, Dam, Dham and Nam to the several parts of the left leg. Pam to the right side, Pham to the left, Bam to the back, Bham to the navel, Mam to the stomach, Yam to the heart, Ram to the right shoulders, Lam to the neek-bone, Vam to the left shoulders, Sam from the heart to the right hand, Sham from the heart to the left hand, Sam from the heart to the right leg, Ham from the heart to the left leg, Lam from the heart to the belly, Ksham from the heart to the mouth.

The Internal Matrika Nyasa.—I bow to the Goddess, representative of all the significant characters, and residing in all the petals of the lotuses whether 2,16,30, 6 or 4 petalled, situated at the anus, penis, abdomen, heart, palate, and forehead, at the tail, in the hairs, with those typified by ড, থ, ক, and চ, and হ২ and ক্ষ২ (in) the vocal organ(22).

To the anus Vam namah, Sam namah, Sham namah, Sam namah; to the organ Vam namah, Bham namah, Mam namah, Lam namah; to the navel, Dam namah, Dham namah, Nam namah, Tam namah, Tham namah, Dam namah, Dham namah, Nam namah, Pam namah, Pham namah; to the heart Kam namah, Kham namah, Gam namah, Gham namah, Nam namah, Cham namah, Chham namah, Jam namah, Jham namah, Nam namah, Tam namah, Tham namah; to the throat Am namah, Am namah, Im namah, Im namah, Um namah, Um namah, Rm namah, Rm namah, Lm namah, Em namah, Aim namah, Om namah, Aum namah, Am namah, Ah namah; to the forehead, Hom namah, Ksham namah.

THE NYASA OF THE PHALANGES.—Om obeisance to Durga in the thumbs, Om Svaha to Durga in the forefingers, Om Vashat to Durga in the middle fingers, Om Hum to Durga the protectress of the elements in the ring fingers, Om Vashat to Durga the saviour in danger in the little fingers. Om phat to the weapons to Durga the saviour in the palms and the backs(23).

THE NYASA OF THE HEARTS.—Om obeisance to Durga in the heart. Om Svaha to Durga in the heart, Om Svaha to Durga in the head, Om Vashat to Durga in the crest, Om Hum to Durga the protectress of the elements in the armour, Om Vashat to Durga the saviour in the three eyes, Om phat to the weapons of Durga. Then thrice make the pranayam with Hrim.

THE PITHA NYASA.—Placing the palms on the heart, Om obeisance to the Sustaining Force, Om obeisance to Prakrti, to Kurma, to Ananta, to the earth, to the ocean of milk, to the white island, to the sphere of jewels, to the kalpa tree, to the crystal seat, to the jewelled throne. On the right shoulder to Dharma, on the left shoulder to Intelligence on the left thigh root, to Resignation, on the right thigh root to Prosperity, on the mouth to Unrighteousness, on the left sight to Ignorance, on the navel to Worldliness, on the right side to Poverty. Once more on the heart Om to Ananta, to Padma; Am to the Solar sphere of twelve phases, Um to the Lunar sphere of sixteen phases, Mam to the Pyric sphere of ten phases, Sam to Purity, Ram to Prosperity, Tam to darkness, Am to the soul,

Am to the innate spirit, Pam to the Divine soul, Hrim to the intellectual soul. In the filaments of the lotus Am to Light, Im to Illusion, Um to Victoria or the goddess of victory, Em to the atoms, Aim to Purity, Om to Felicity, Aum to Beauty, Am to Glory, Ah to the giver of all success. Above the lotus Hum phat to the adamantine clawed and toothed weapons, the great throne(24).

Then make the Dhyana or meditate on the figure of the Goddess in the following manner. Om with locks of hair, braided and flowing, and the forehead ornamented by the crescent moon, with three eyes, with a face equal to the full moon in brightness, with a complexion of molten gold, well-formed and lovely-eyed, full of the freshness of youth, decorated will all kinds of ornaments, with a set of pearly teeth, Devi, with a breast compact and full, gracefully bent at three places, Destroyer of the Buffalo Demon, with ten arms as soft and well rounded as the stalks of lotus, holding a trident on the right, a sword and a discus from upwards, a sharp arrow, and a dart in the right hand, a shield, a bent bow, a noose, a goad, and a bell or an axe. Under her lies a headless Buffalo carcass, whence rises the demon with a sword in hand, pierced in his heart by the Devi's trident, his lungs drawn out, his body besmeared with blood, and eye balls distended encircled by the serpent noose, presenting a face made terrific by contracted eyes, brows and frowns, the noose with the fore-locks of the demon held by Durga in her left hand, while the Devi's lion is described with a mouth tainted red, the right foot of the Goddess resting evenly on the back of the lion, and the toe of the left foot a little higher on the shoulders of the demon. Om serene-faced Goddess, sub-duer of the pride of Daityas and Danavas ! Om this representation of the Goddess is worshipped and prayed by the immortals. Om the Goddess is always surrounded by Ugrachanda, Prachanda, Chandogra, Chandanayika, Chanda, Chandavati Chandarupa and Atichandika, the eight Saktis Om contemplate the mother of the world for the attainment of virtue, all wishes, and beautitude. Then place on the head a flower and worship the goddess with spiritual offerings(25) in the following manner. Meditate the Devi in the lotus of the heart, and offer the Padya (water for washing the feet) from the receptacle in the stamina with the nectar from the lotus of the heart. Then present the mind as an arghya, and to the mouth of the goddess apply the ambrosial water exuding from the water-pot of a thousand-petalled lotus. Offer frankincense of the twenty-five essences of nature, and present the flowers of harmlessness, of intelligence, of forbearance, of mercy, of contentment, of knowledge, unenviousness, of non-illusiveness, of pridelessness, of impassionateness, of uninimicalness, and of the twelve organs of the body. Then offer the lamp of elemental fire, the incense of elemental air, the chauri of space, the mirror of the sun, the umbrella of the moon, the heart-strings as the girdle, and felicity as the best necklace, and the inward pulsation as the ringing bell. Present the ocean as the draught of water, the mountains as meat, and the ether which fills the universe as frumenty. And mental dancing and singing which come from the six Muses(26) complete the worship.

Then establish the special arghya :—Describe on the left a triangle and worship it by a flower with Om to the Sustaining Force. Place upon the triangle the tripod and wash the conchshell with Phat and on the tripod put the conchshell and fill three-fourths of it with water and deposit in it durva, ricec handan, and flowers. Then while repeating the following words pour drops of water in the conch-shell : Ksham, Lam, Ham, Sam, Sham, Sam, Vam, Lam, Ram, Yam, Mam, Bham, Bam,

Pham, Pam, Nam, Dham, Dam, Tham, Tam, Nam, Dham, Dam, Tham, Tam, Nam, Jham, Jam Chham, Cham, Nam, Gham, Gam, Kham, Kam, Ah, Am, Aum, Om, Aim, Em Lm Lm Rm Rm Um, Um, Im, Im, Am, Am, Mam. Then worship the tripod, Mam obeisance to the sphere of Fire of ten phases: the conchshell, Am obeisance to the solar sphere of twelve phases and: the water, Um obeisance to the lunar sphere of sixteen phases. With the goad mudra contemplate the several tirthas and invoke them from the Solar sphere thus, Om Ganga &c.

Then worship Surya, Ganesa, Vishnu, Seva, and Durga, and the nine planets, commencing from the sun and once more meditate on Durga. Then invoke her from her seat in the heart by the mantras, Om Durga Devi approach, Om Durga Devi approach, stay here, stay! cover the fore-fingers with Hum, present the Galini Mudra, and with Vam and the dhenu-mudra, observe the water in the conchshell with Vaushat, perform the Nyasa to the six parts of the body. Hram obeisance to the heart, Hrim Svaha to the head, Hrum Vashat to the crest, Hraim Hum to the armour, Hraum Vaushat to the three eyes, Hruh phat to the weapons, to the palms and the back: Meditating on the water of the conchshell as Durga and worshipping the same with Chandan, flowers &c., and covering the same with fish mudra repeat eight times the Mulamantra.

Repeat the Mulamantra several times and offer handsful of flowers anointed with chandan. Then with the water from the arghy-pot finish the Japa and repeat, Om you are the repository of our secrets, inmost secrets, receive the Japa performed by me, oh! Devi, may you bless me with prosperity and success! Then offer water on the right hand of the Devi.

Then on the four sides of the Ghata fix four arrows with the mantras, Om from Kandas (arrow) Om from Kandas (arrow) grow hardness upon hardness, may he [who dares trespass within sacred precincts] be pierced as if with a thousand blades of Durva, which grow one over the other. Encircle the same with three threads with the following mantra, Om with the thread the heavens and the earth are encircled, by me similarly this place is encircled, may the serpents protect this place from all impurities &c. Again with mustard repeat the following: Om Vetalas &c. Om the obtruders, the obstructives, the heretics, the nagas, the enemies of sacrifices, the blood-thirsty, may they be destroyed by these mustards, which shall pierce them as if with a thunderbolt.

Next offer the silver seat by first purifying it with a flower and water, and thrice repeating Vam, Om obeisance to the silver seat, Om this chandan and flower to its lord Vishnu, Om to the donee of this my obeisance, Om Hrim this silver seat to Durga, the destroyer of the sacrifice of Daksha, the most terrible, surrounded by a million of yoginis, thou Bhadrakali.

Then offer a brazen pot filled with water for washing the feet of Durga and arghya, previously established, chandan with the cup, flowers, a garland, a pair of clothes, dhupa incense, a lamp, water for drinking in brass tumblers, water for washing in pots, water for bathing in large brazen pots, and then rice and fruits and other edibles and betel leaves, spices and nuts &c. &c., and lastly a bed with the bedstead.

In this way the Goddess is worshipped every morning from pratipada to the sixth day of the moon. One of the officiating priests reads the Devimahatmya(27) from the Markandeya Purana, aud the tantradharaka helps the pujaka priest in the worship. A separate priest is appointed to repeat the mula *mantra* a hundred thousand times, and he is called the japaka. In some houses the pujaka after finishing the puja commences the homa. After the puja every forenoon and evening the usual arati(28) is made. This is offering a series of lights to the goddess, and moving the same in graceful curves before her, accompanied by music &c. In the evening offerings of sweet-meats are daily made. In some families every day from the Kalparambha a goat is sacrificed.

THE BODHANA.

THE arousing of the Goddess may be performed either on the ninth day of the moon preceding the new moon of Asvina, or on the sixth day of the following. On the evening of the sixth on the Vel tree the Devi is awakened, Narayana is worshipped, and the sankalpa is made in the manner described above with the following words, Om on the Vel tree as a part of the annual autumnal Durga Puja, I having worshipped the ganapati and other devas invoke and invite Durga, and perform the preliminary ceremony(29) adhivasa. After scattering mustard, establishing the ordinary arghya, and performing the bhutasuddhi, and asanasuddhi and the several Nyasas in the manner described above and having worshipped Surya, Ganesa and other Gods address the vel tree, Om vilva tree come hither; Om this flower to vilva tree. Then worship Durga in the vilva tree, and making the usual dhyan worship her with sixteen kinds of offerings. Then rouse Devi, and, touching the north-eastern twig of the tree, repeat, " Aim for the destruction of Ravana and for the success of Rama, Brahma had in earlier days at an unseasonable time awakened thee ; I, also on the eve of the sixth lunar day of Asvina, do arouse thee. Indra having so aroused thee gained dominion and the heavens ; therefore do I arouse thee with a view to obtain superhuman dominion and transcendental power. As the ten-faced was destroyed by Rama so may I have might to destroy my enemies." Then in the vilva tree the Devi is invited. " Om Sri fruit tree, thou art always gratifying to Amvika, thou art born on the top of mounts Meru, Mandara, Kailas, and Himavat, thou art born on the top of Sri mountain, thou art prosperous fruit, thou art the dwelling-place of health and prosperity, thou art by me deputed, oh ! dost thou go, thou art the likeness of Durga ! Thou art born from the vedas and the vedangas, oh Sri tree thou art gratifying to Chandika, I am inviting her for worship, dost thou give me thy twig." This inviting is followed by music and arati. Then tie together with a twine of white Clitoria ternata the nine plants *viz.* plantain, turmeric, sesbania, vilva, pomegranate, colocasia antiquorum, jonesia asoka, colocasia indica, and paddy plant, these nine form the Navapatrica. Taking oil and turmeric-powder anoint the Navapatrica with a vedic mantra; also touch her with the following auspicious articles, chandan, earth, pebble, paddy, Durva grass, flower, nutmeg, curd, ghi, svastica(30), virmillion, conchshell, collyrium, the gorochana, mustard, gold, silver, copper, the chamara, a mirror, a light, and a broad plate. Each of these articles is graced with a separate vedic mantra. The Navapatrica is thrice touched with each of the articles and thrice the same articles are placed on the earth. Having thus finished the adhivasa of the Navapatrica, similar adhivasa of the pratima is performed, and a yellow-stained thread with Durva grass is tied round the left wrist of Durga. The whole ceremony of adhivasa is completed by an arati of the idols.

SAPTIMI,(31).

THIS IS the first-day of the puja. The programme of the day is, 1stly bathing the Navapatrica, 2ndly vivifying the idols by invoking the several gods and goddesses represented by them, 3rdly anointing them with several drugs and cosmetics, 4thly the worship of the principal gods, 5thly sacrifice, the 6thly the institution of the

Homa fire, if not previously done, 7thly the Homa or the offering of oblations to the sacred fire, and 8thly worship of the minor gods. The day's, work is closed by worshipping a virgin of the Brahman caste (Kumari).

Early in the morning having finished their morning ceremonies the priests enter the place of worship,and taking out the Navapatrica they either carry it to the river-side to have it bathed,or bathe it in the courtyard of the house according to the family custom. But the taking to the river-side does not interefere with once more bathing the Navapatrica on the court-yard with the drugs and cosmetics mentioned above, where that instance prevails. The priests then approach the vilva tree and make the usual sankalpa, and with mustard seeds the pujaka prays Om may the woods and the forests protect us, for I sprinkle with water the vaishnavas, Om may the woods and the forests protect us, for I shield the vishnavas, Om may the woods and the forests protect us, for I adore the Vaishnavi ! Om may the woods and the forests protect us, for I offer the Ahuti to the Vaishnavi. Om thou art a vaishnava, Om you are all vaishnavas, and therefore do you protect me. The priests next worship the gods Surya, Ganesa, &c.,

offer chandan and oil and turmeric to the vilva tree, also rice, incense &c., anoint that branch of the vilva tree with turmeric and oil, which bears a pair of fruits, and touching the same invoke Om vilva tree you are most prosperous, you are always welcome to Sankara, I worship Durga, having taken a branch of yours, oh lord, forgive the pain generated by the separation of the branch, for it is said the gods have worshipped Durga on your branch, I bow to the vilva tree born on the Himavat, favourite of Parvati and embraced by Siva. You are auspicious in action and a favourite of Bhagavati, for the sake of Bhavani's words give me all success. Then with a sharp sword the priests sever the branch uttering these words, Om phat sever, sever phat, svaha, Om for the increase of children, life, and wealth I take thee away, oh beloved of Chandika, seated on this branch, dost thou grant me wealth and dominion. Welcome oh DeviChandika for our prosperity, accept our pujah, beautiful-faced, I bow to you, oh spouse of Sankara, Om Sriphala tree thou art born on the mountain Mandar, Meru, Kailasa and on the top of the Himavat, thou art always a favourite of Amvica. Born on the top of Sri hill, Sriphala, thou art the above of prosperity, I take thee away to worship thee as

Durga herself. The twig so severed is then placed in the Navapatrica, and the entire bundle is carried to the courtyard, the drums beating and music playing. The Navapatrica is placed upon a decorated seat, and the Sankalpa for establishing and bathing her is made.

SNANA(32).—The Navapatrica is anointed with oil and turmeric with the following mantra. Om Devi you are variously shaped and veiled with good clothes, by anointing you all my fears are extinguished. Then taking a conchshell full of pure water, the Navapatrica is bathed nine times with the following mantras; Om thou resident on the plantain tree, and on the bosom of Vishnu, I bow to thee oh Navapatrica I bow to thee oh Chandanayika. Om this water for bathing Hrim to Durga who resides in the Navapatrica. Om thou art kachvi, thou art a resident of the earth, and a constant giver of success. Dost thou as Durga give us success everywhere in virtue of this bathing. Om Haridra, thou art the representative of Hara, always a favourite of Sankara, Oh Devi thou art Rudra's self, give me peace everywhere. Om Jayanti, thou art the Goddess of Victory, and dispenser of victories all the world over, I do hereby anoint thee, dost thou give victory in my house. Om Sriphala thou art the resting place of Sri and the augmentor of success. Mayst thou inspire me with good intentions, mayst thou be ever pleased. Om Dadimi, thou destroyst the sins and always appeasest the hunger of the world, thou art created as a fruit, best thou gratified oh beloved of Hara. Om Asoka be stable and dost thou destroy our sorrows, oh Durga, thou art worshipped by me and be thou therefore stable. Om Mana,(33) thou art respected by the Suras and the Asuras in the mana tree, I bathe thee, oh Mahadevi, dost thou grant me honor. Om Lakshmi, thou art represented as rice, thou art the giver of life to the living, dost thou become stable and fulfil our wishes by never ceasing thy benign presence.

Then with river water the priests anoint the Navapatrica with the following mantra, Om Atreyi, Bharati, Ganga, Jamuna, and Sarasvati, Saraju,Gandaki, Punya, Svetaganga, and Kausiki, Om Bhogavati from the nether-worlds and Mandakini from the heavens, may all these respectfully bathe you. May the Suras, may Vishnu, Brahma and Mahesvara, Vasudeva, Jagannatha, also lord Sankarshana, Pradyumna, and Anirudha, who confer success, Indra, and lord Agni, Jama and Nirti, Varuna,and Pavana, and the lord of wealth, also Siva, Sesha with Brahma, the Dikpalas, may all these anoint you. Om may Fame, Prosperity, Felicity, and Peace, Contentment, and Glory, and the Matris anoint you with the well associated Dharmapala. Om may Aditya, the Moon, Mercury, Mars, Jupiter, and Venus, and Saturn and the planets with Rahu and Ketu anoint you. Om may the Rshis, the Munis, and the cows, the Devamatris, the Devapatnis, the fixed stars, the Nagas, the daityas and the apsaras, the weapons, all the missiles, the kings, the conveyances, the wonderful medicines, and the signs of the time, the water-places, the seas, the hills, the holy places, the cataracts, and the clouds and rivers, the devas, the danavas, the gandharvas, the jakshas, and the rakshas, the elephants and others may anoint you for the attainment of virtue and wishes. Om may Sindhu, Bhairavi, and Sona and those lakes which lie on this earth all with one respectful obeisance anoint you with water. Om may those Nagas commencing with Takshaka, who live in the netherworld all with respectful salutations anoint you. Om may the oceans(34) of salt, of sugarcane juice, of wine, of ghi, of curd, of milk and of other waters, the seven oceans and others anoint you. Then with water from a conchshell Om the lord of all the devas named Isana, Sulapani and Mahadeva anoint you with water. Then with Ganga water(35) Om with that water which is from the Mandakini, and which is good and purifier of all sins, which is the Vishnu torrent in the heavens, may your bathing be with it. With warm water(36) Om water that is purified, superior, and warm, filled with the force of fire and life, destroyer of all sins I anoint you. With the water perfumed with sandal wood Om full of fragrance, beautiful, cool, good-looking, giver of all happiness, with such water I anoint you. With water perfumed by flowers(37) Om for the sake of dignity with unboiled drugs of Asvini cumaras, and with the splendour of Brahma I anoint you, Om for our strength with the drugs of the river Sarasvati and capturing the spirit of the same I anoint you, Om for power, for prosperity, for fame, and renown with the spirits of the essences I anoint you. With honey with a vedic mantra. With water sweetened by sugar with the Gayatri mantra. With milk with a vedic mantra. Hrum Vashat to the forelock. With ghee and a vedic mantra Hraim Hrum to the armour. With curd and a vedic mantra, Hraum Vaushat to the eyes. With cocoanut water Hrum phat to the weapons. With the five Gabyas(38) Am to the heart. With water of Kusagrass and a vedic mantra. With chandan water and a vedic hymn Om to Haimavati. With Sarvaushadhi and Mahaushadhi and a Sama Hymn. With juice of sugarcane and the Bhagavati Gayatri, Om to Bhagavati. With the five tonics, Om to the messengers of Siva. With rain water, Om Hrim to Chamunda. With water perfumed by camphor, Hrim to Maya. With water perfumed by red sandal-wood, Hrim to Parvati. With infusion of Kakkol and with a Sukta, Hrim to Chandika. With water purified by a sword, Hrim to Gauri. With water purified by gold, Om you were born gold-colored on the earth for the success of the Devas, oh Mahesvari I bathe you with this divine water. With water purified by silver, Hrim to Durga. Hrim to Aparna with Garochana. Hrim to Mahesvari with saffron water. Hrim to Amvica with water perfumed by Sriphala leaves. Hrim to Durga, with perfumed oil. Hrim to Chandika with sesamum oil. Hrim to Narayani with Narayana oil. Hrim to Chamunda with vishnu oil. Om to Chandika with the water from various holy rivers, and with the hymn, Om with that water which is reputed to be the life of all beings, I bathe Bhagavati Durga, may she be propitiated. With the water of the tank, Om with this water which is collected from the hills[39] I bathe you oh Parvati. Om to Hingulavasini with water purified by pearls. Om to Durga with water purified with coral. Om to Devi with lake water. Om Hrim to Bhagavati with earth from the river-side. Om Hrim to Durga with earth dug up by the tusk of a wild boar[40]. Om Hrim to Katyayani with earth from the doors of prostitutes. Om Hrim to Atichandika with earth from the doors of a Prince. Om Hrim to Gauri with earth dug up by the horns of a bull. Om Hrim to Annapurna with earth from the doors of a temple. Om Hrim to Parvati with earth from the shores of the ocean. Om Hrim to Narayani with earth from anthills. Om Hrim to Sarvapapaharini with earth from the shores of the Ganga. Hrim to Bhuvanesvari with earth from a quadrivium. Om Hrim with water dropped from a millefluent. Om the oceans, the lakes, the heavenly streams with Sarvoushadhi and purifying water, I bathe you Om with the waters from the seven oceans. Then the priests bathe the goddess with four jars of water with four mantras from the four vedas.

Then singing in the Gandhar mode[41] and beating the kettle drum, the Navapatrica is bathed with a jar of Ganga water and with the following mantra, Om the gods Brahma, Vishnu, Siva and others lave you with the first jar filled with heavenly Ganga water. Singing in the Vibhasha mode accompanied with Deva music she is bathed with the second jar filled with rain-water. Om Suresvari the Maruts pour over you with devotional cantos the second jar filled with water from the clouds. With Bhairavi mode and Bhim music, Om Indra and other gods and Lokapalas bathe you with the third jar filled with sea water. With Lalita mode and vijaya music, Om the Vidyadharas bathe you the best of goddesses with the fourth jar filled with water from the Sarasvati river. With Korada mode and Indrabhisheka music, Om the Nagas bathe you with the fifth jar filled with water perfumed by the pollens of lotus. With Badari mode and conchshell music, Om the Himavat and the Hemakuta and other mountains bathe you with the sixth jar filled with water from a cataract. With Vasanta mode and Pancham music, Om the Rshis bathe you oh Suresvari with the seventh jar filled with water from holy places. With Dhamasi mode and Bhairavi music, Om the eight vasus bathe you with the eighth jar of water perfumed with musk and sandalwood. The priest concludes by saying, I salute thee, oh Durga, with eight kinds of prosperity.

Avahana. Then the priest offers flowers to the Bhutas,&c. and with mustard and lajac(42) worships the Bhutas and as described above performs the Bhutasuddhi. He next wipes Navapatrica with a new napkin and dresses it with a silk cloth and takes it to the place of worship and places, it to the right of the idols. Then touching the seat of the idols he recites Om Chandika stir stir, move, move oh Durga, enter the house of worship, enter oh Devi my house with thy eight saktis. Oh lovely-faced receive my offerings for the promotion of my prosperity. He also moves the idol a little and places her facing south or the east with various songs and music. Om Aim, Hrim, sedeo, sede, sedite tu mater !

The priest then places in the usual form a ghata before Durga, and another before the Navapatrica, and after establishing the ordinary Arghya and performing the Bhutasuddhi, Asanasuddhi, Matrika Nyasa, &c., and such other preliminaries as are already described fixes the kandas (arrows) and encircles them with thread.

The priest next meditates the form of Durga as described above and worships her with mental offerings. Then making another arghya addresses her. Om Durga Devi hither advance, hither proceed, stay here, be seated here, and makes representations of certain Mudras &c. &c.

The priest now invokes the goddess by placing the right hand on her breast and recites, Om Welcome Devi to my house with thy eight Saktis, accept my worship done according to the sastras, oh dispenser of all blessings, oh lotus-eyed, I perform this autumnal festival,respond to me, oh great goddess, the destroyer of demoniac powers. Annihilator of all transgressions in this unfordable ocean of the world, save me blessed goddess, I salute thee beloved of Sankara. Protect my life, my honor, my offsprings, wives, and wealth. As thou art the only defender of all, oh goddess, the most beloved in the world, enter and stay in this sacrifice as long as I am worshipping thee, Devi, delight of Menaka confer on me success. I invoke thee goddess in the earthen idol, and in the Sriphala twig ; descend Devi from tha peaks of Kailasa, Vindya, and the Himalya Mountains. Come, come, oh fortunate mother, destroy my enemies and grant me victory. I adore thee with respect, oh nova dea, adored by the gods with fruit-bearing twigs and branches. Oh Devi residing in the foliage accept my offerings, and be gratified Devi Durga approach and will presence in this vicinity. Oh lotus-eyed Devi receive this autumnal offering. Supreme goddess Chandi, I invoke the gods and goddesses, who move about the spheres graciously, may you alight on these figures and be sustained by them. Oh! propitious lady of the world protect us for ever; to thee I bow. Advance, oh goddess Chandika, thou cause of all prosperity, oh lovely-faced Devi accept my offerings, I bow to thee beloved of Sankara.

Then the right eye is vivified. The gourd sacrifice is lavated with water and decorated with vermillion and the priest exclaims, Om to Durga this gourd sacrifice. Om wonderful are the eyes of the gods, the eyes of Mitra, those of Agni, those of Varuna they comprehend the heavens and the earth and they penetrate endless space. Om the Sun is the light of the world. The left eye is similarly vivified by another vedic hymn. The eye on the forehead is also vivified by another hymn. Then touching the breast of the idol the priest, recites five vedic mantras. The idol is vivified with the following, Om of the mantras for vivifying Durga, the rshis are Brahma, Vishnu and Mahesvara, the metres are Rig, Yajus and Sama, the god is vital force, and these are used in vivifying idols. Om Am Hrim Kraum Yam Ram Lam Sam Sham Sam Haum Ham Sah of this Sri Durga, these are the vital breaths.

Om Am Hrim Kraum Yam Ram Lam Sam Sham Sam Haum Ham Sah the life of Durga be here seated. Om Am Hrim &c., so be also the organs of Durga, Om Am &c., the voice, the mind, the eyes, the ears, the nose, the heart take possession of this idol for ever *Svaha*. The priest next recites another hymn by touching the cheeks, Om the lives of these be here established, Om the lives of these be here moving, Om let these be deified Svaha. Then on the breast of the Devi, performs the Matrika Nyasa.

In this manner the lives of the nine plants in the Navapatrica are established.

PUJA.

THEN follow these ceremonies : Contemplate the form of the deity as described above, and sprinkle over the silver seat the water from the ordinary arghya established before. Om Bam to the silver seat. Salutation to Vishnu its lord. Salutation to the donee Hrim Durga. Then touching the seat, Om Chamunda the beloved of Hara accept this jewelled seat. Om Hrim Durga oh Durga the Saviour Svaha. Om this seat to the destroyer of the sacrifice of Daksha, to the most terrific, to her who is surrounded by a million of yoginis, to Bhadrakali. This seat lorded by Chandra

Hrim to Durga. Prosperous Durga welcome, most welcome. Then interrogate her about her health.

The padya should consist of Hibiscus rosasinesis, durvagrass, lotus, and Clitoria ternata. After purifying the same in the manner prescribed above the priest exclaimes Om great goddess, receive this padya, oh destroyer of all misery save me, oh propitious Devi, salutation be to thee spouse of Sankara. And with the Daksha yajna &c., mantra, this padya lorded by Varuna is dedicated to Hrim Durga.

Arghya is next made on the conchshell pot with chandan, flowers, rice, barley, Kusa grass, sesamun, mustard, durva, and vilva leaves. Holding the conchshell the priest recites Om the beloved of Hara receive this arghya beautifully established on a conch shell with durva and other offerings. And with the Daksha yajna &c. mantra this arghya lorded by Prajapati Hrim Svaha to Durga.

Then water with jasmine flower, cloves, and kakkol is offered for washing. Om the water from Mandakini, prosperous and purifier of all sins, is offered to thee, receive this, oh goddess &c., with the usual mantra, Om this water for washing lorded by Varuna Hrim Svadha to Durga.

Madhuparka(43) Om Mahadavi, this confection

of honey invented by Brahma &c. receive this, oh Paramesvari, by me to thee offered reverentially. Om this confection of honey with the pot lorded by Prajapati &c. Hrim Svaha to Durga.

Then once more water for washing. Om this cool, transparent, pure, eternal, and beautiful water is offered by me with love, receive this, oh Durga. Om this water for bathing lorded by Varuna Hrim &c.

Om this silk cloth made of numerous threads and of threads got out of coccoons, this white cloth receive thee, oh the best of women. Om Durga, receive this many-colored cloth, and wear it as a spring dress. Om Hrim &c. lorded by Vrhaspati &c.

Om these bangles cut out of conchshells beautiful and born in the ocean, these auspicious ornaments for thy wrists accept oh Durga and be pleased. Om embossed with good jewels as bright as the sun or fire, these personal ornaments accept them oh lady of the gods these ornaments lorded by the moon &c.

Om unknown is thy body to me, but accept these cosmetics by me offered and anoint thy body with these cosmetics lorded by Gandharva &c.

Om these beautiful fragrant god-made flowers, pleasing to the heart, sweet-scented are offered by me oh goddess accept them. These flowers lorded by Vanaspati &c.

Om this incense derived from the juices of plants, the food of Gandharvas and gods, accept them, oh Devi, they are offered with respect by me. This incense lorded by Vanaspati &c.

Om the light of fire, the light of the sun, the light of the lightning, and the light of the stars, oh Durga the best of all lights, receive this lamp offered by me. Thou art the light of the sun, the light of the moon, the light of electricity, the light of fire, thou art indeed the fountain of all light, accept this lamp. This lamp lorded by Agni &c.

Om salutation to the omnipresent goddess, salutation to the beloved of Sankara, oh Devi this collyrium for eyes is offered, accept &c.

Om these fruits and roots grown in villages and forests, of various flavour and of various tastes, oh Devi accept, soon &c.

Om this unboiled rice with ghee, fruits, and sweetmeats together with betels are offered by me accept oh Devi these offerings &c.

Om this rice, the giver of life, with curries of six different tastes variously spiced and carefully cooked, oh Devi, accept these because, they are delicious &c.

Om rice boiled with ghee made of cow milk,

and decocted with several sweets by me offered with love, accept this payasa &c.

Om made with several sweets, well formed and variously shaped, several kinds of cakes, oh Devi, accept them for my sake &c.

Om these balls of sweetmeats, best and well confected with sugar are offered by me, accept these, oh goddess &c.

Om this delicious milk, well-boiled, and mixed with several sweets and spices, this giver of life nutritious and healthful potation, accept oh Devi &c.

Om this *laddu* tasteful, confected with ghi and molasses is offered by me accept oh Devi &c.

Then chipitaka, (flattened rice), and cocoanut, offered with the mula mantra.

Om Parmesvari, accept this water for drink, cold, beautiful, perfumed with camphor and several fragrances, and pure, Hrim &c.

Then water for washing the face is offered with Om accept this cold, perfumed, crystal water by me respectfully given, oh Devi &c.

Om this vermillion, beautifying paint, giver of long life to one's husband, is offered by me with love, accept oh spouse of Hara, accept this &c.

Om this betel consisting of leaves and fruits and several spices is offered, accept oh Devi &c.

Om this dessert dish filled with various fruits, flowers, and, other charming articles is offered by me, oh lovely goddess, accept it &c.

Om this collection of 108 choice blades of Durva, accept, oh Devi, salutation be to thee who art Felicity. Obeisance to thee, oh Omnipresent, Devi, and giver of happiness and final beatitude &c.

Om this wreath of Shriphala leaves, born of nectar and full of prosperity, always a favorite with Mahadeva, oh Prosperous and Pure Devi, I offer this to thee &c.

Om this beautiful and charming garland of several fragrant flowers put together by a thread is offered to thee, accept it. Then the speculum mirror is presented and the sacrifice offered.

Then three handsful of flowers are offered with the usual Dhyan.

THE SACRIFICE (44).

Let the priest be seated with his face towards the north and the sacrificial animal facing east, and let him perform the following ceremonies :

Observe the animal and recite Om phat to the weapon. Om Agni was an animal, of whom a sacrifice was made, which procured him this habitation, the same will be thine where

Agni is; him shalt thou conquer; now drink this water. Om Vayu was an animal &c., Om Surya was an animal &c., Om Varahi, Yamuna, Ganga, Karatoya, Sarasvati, Kaveri, Chandrabhaga, and Sindhu, Bhairava, and the seas, Sarayu, Gandaki, Punya, Kausiki and Mahesa, approach for the ablution of the goat.

Om I purify thy words, and I purify thy life, Om I purify thy eyes, Om I purify thy ears, Om I purify thy navel, Om I purify thy jaws, Om I purify thy organs, Om I purify thy habits. Om thy mind be purified, Om thy words be puriified, Om thy hearing be purified, Om thy life be purfied, Om thy sight be purified. Om purified be whatever malignant in thee. Om be thee same blessed, Om be thee same pure, Om pure art thou Svaha. Sprinkle water over the goat.

Om tie the animal, fix the animal between pillars as dark as the clouds. Om be the animal with horns and other limbs. Om secure the animal to the pillar which divides life from death, creation from chaos. Om secure, fix the animal which represents in part the universe. Hrah Phat Svaha, Om Hram Hrim Hrum Cham to Chandika. This animal still I own, Om this fragrant flower with chandan and other articles of worship to the goat animal. Om loosen the animal with its horns and other limbs, set free the animal, Svaha. Om pardon me! Apply virmillion paste on its forehead. Om this padya to the goat animal, similarly offer other edibles. Om salutation to the goat animal. Om salutation to its lord Agni. Om salutation to its donee Hrim Durga. Then after throwing some flowers on the goat, worship the Gods residing in its several limbs. Om to Rudhiravadana in the head, Om to Sangini in the forehead, Om to Srnga between the eye-brows, Om to Trinetra in the eyes, Om to Parvati in the ears, Om to Gauri in the nostrils, Om to Chandika in the chin Om to Ugrachandika in the sets of teeth, Om Chandaghanta in the tongue, Om to Virupaksha in the mouth, Om to Chanda in the neck. Om to Mahabhairavi in the back, Om to Vaishnavi in the belly, Om to Chandapriya in the fore-feet, Om to Sarvesvari in the sides, Om to Virupaksha in the waist, Om to Kausiki in the hoofs, Om Praharshini in the tail. And Om to the other Gods in the other parts of the body.

Once more observe the animal and address Om goat, blessed be my star that thou hast appeared as a sacrificial animal, I salute thee and all such forms of sacrifice, Om salutation to thou object of sacrifice. Om all misfortunes of the donor are removed by the gratification of Chandika. I salute thee, oh Vaishnavi in the form of sacrifice. Om the animals are created by the Self-born Himself for sacrifice, and therefore do I kill thee in this yajna though thou art unkillable. Om thou art born in the womb of animal for the sacred purposes of puja, homa, and other ceremonies. Be the goddess propitiated with thy flesh mixed with blood.

Then place flowers on the head of the sacrifice with Aim Hrim Srim, and make the usual sankalpa. To the ear of the animal address the following, Om *hili hili, kili, kili,* variously formed, Haim Haim this goat animal, may salvation be granted to it, Svaha. Also repeat the animal gayatri to the ear of the beast.

Bring out the sword and upon it describe with virmillion paste Hrim, and contemplating it, adore the sword god, Om sombre, spear-handed, the very self of kalaratri, excited, red-eyed, red-faced, red-wreathed, red-clothed, noose-handed, blood-thirsty sword I salute thee. Thou art the tongue of Chandika and the gratifier of the gods. Then offer chandan, flowers, &c. to the sword, and worship the several gods presiding over several parts of the sword. Om to Mahadeva in the handle, Om to Yama in the edge, Om sword with eight-fold names Visasan &c. derived from Brahma I salute thee. Thou art the asterism Krtiks, and hast Mahesvara for thy lord, thy body is gold, thy maker is Janardana. Thou art our father, grand father and lord, defend me forever. Thou art colored as blue cloud, thy teeth are sharp, and thy waist is narrow. Thy form is a graceful curve, and thou art furious and most mighty. Offer flowers with Om, Phat salutation to the sharp-toothed sword. Then hold the sword with the following mantra, Om salutation be to Kali, Kali, Devi, the goddess of thunderbolt, and the holder of iron club. Om Hrim Kali Kali, oh terrible-teethed, sphem, sphem, phet-karini, devour, swallow, sever, kill, destroy all the evil-doers, despatch this beast, cut him up by the sword, cut, cut, kili, kili, chiki, chiki, drink up, drink the blood, sphoum, sphoum, kiri kiri, Om salutation to Durga. Having with this mantra inspired the sword, give a handful of flowers, Om sword, thou severer, thou scimitar, sharp-edged destroyer, I bow to thee, mother Prosperity, I bow to Victoria and to the Defender of the Faith. With Om Hrim Phat take up the shining sword in hand and apply it on the shoulders of the beast.

The sacrifice is taken to the courtyard of the house, where a Y-shaped post is fixed. Between the sacrificial post and the Devi is placed on a cleaned spot an entire leaf of plantain under which the root Hrim and the triangular Yantra are described. Upon the leaf is placed a shallow earthen vessel commonly called Kharpar, with the following articles for blood sacrifice, *viz.*, rock salt, honey, sugar, a betel nut and a ripe plantain and the amimal is then despatched with one blow. In this pot a small quantity of the blood from the sacrifice is put and a bit of flesh from the trunk of the beast, care being taken that no bits of hair be present. Then the sankalpa for presenting this blood is made: Om Aim Hrim Srim Kausiki be satiated with blood. Om salutation to this blood of goat, Om this blood of a goat to prosperous Durga. On the head of the animal a light is placed and the head with the light is offered to the goddess. Om salutation to this head of a goat with a light on it. A sankalpa is again made for offering this head to the goddess. Om this head with the light I offer to Durga. Then dividing the blood in the earthen dish into four parts, Om salutation to Vidarika in the south-east corner. Om to Paparakshasi in the south-west corner. Om to Putana in the north-west corner. Om to Kalika in the north-east corner.

Then pray to the goddess as follows: Om three-eyed, terrible-faced, skull-wreathed goddess, thou art the destroyer of all asuras, thou holder of sword and club, oh destroyer of the buffalo demon, oh Mahamaya, oh suppressor of the pride of all daityas, I give this sacrifice of goat, accept it, oh beloved of Hara. Oh Kalaratri having received this sacrifice be satisfied, oh Mahakali protect me Devi Chandika. Om Kali Kali and Mahakali, the destroyer of our sins accept this sacrifice with its blood and confer blessing on us, left eyed Goddess. Then offer handsful of flower and with music and cheers make the arati. Taking a drop of the blood apply it on the forehead and recite, Om may those whom I touch by my feet, Om may those whom I see with my eyes be subdued by me, if they be my enemies. Om Aim Srim Svaha.

Then show the mirror to the goddess and swing the chauri and make the Arati with music and all kinds of drum instruments.

THE WORSHIP OF THE NAVAPATRICA.

Om salutation be to the goddess residing in the nine branches. Om Rambha Devi approach, you are welcome. Om salutation be to Brahmani the goddess dwelling in the plantain tree. Om Devi Durga welcome, come near us. In the Brahma form distribute peace to all. Om salutations be to you :

Om, salutation be to Kalika, the goddess dwelling in the Arum plant. Om, good-natured in the war of Mahisha demon you became arum plant. Om, the beloved of Hara, come hither for my blessing.

Om, salutation be to Durga, the goddess dwelling in the turmeric plant. Om, Haridra, you are Hara incarnate. Om, good-natured you are Uma incarnate. For the destruction of my ill-luck do receive my poojah and be propitiated.

Om, salutation be to Kartiki, the goddess, dwelling iu the Sesbania plant. Om, during the destruction of Sumbha and Nisumbha demons, goddess of success, you were worshipped by Indra and all gods. Be plaaesd with us.

Om, salutation be to Siva, the goddess, dwelling in the vilva tree. Om, beloved of Mahadeva and beloved of Vishnu, beloved of Uma, vilva tree, I salute you.

Om, salutation be to Raktadantika (bloodteethed,) the goddess, dwelling in the pomegranate tree. Om, formerly in the war, you became

Dadima in the presence of Raktavija demon, you acted the part of Uma, therefore bless us.

Om, salutation be to Sokarahita (devoid of sorrow,) the goddess dwelling in the Asoka trec. Om, Asoka tree, you please Siva and you destroy all sorrow. Make me sorrowless in the same way as you please Durga.

Om, salutation be to Chamunda, the goddess dwelling in the Mana tree. Om, on whose leaves rests the Devi, beloved of Sachi, for my prosperity receive my puja.

Om, salutations be to Lakshmi, the goddess, dwelling in the rice plant. Om, for the preservation of the life of all beings you were created by Brahma. Om, preserve me in the same way as you please Uma.

Om salutation be to Durga dwelling in the nine plants. Then offer to the nine, the sixteen articles of worship as described above with a separate bedstead to each. Then salute the nine together, Om plants you are nova dea, charming to Mahadeva, receive all the offerings and protect me.

Then the sixty-four yoginies(45) are worshipped. Each is invoked by name and established. Each is separately addressed and each receives a separate set of offerings.

Then the Japa is made and it is offered to Durga with the mantra mentioned above.

Vishnu is next worshipped with sixteen offerings, the three ghatas are worshipped, so are Ganesa, Lakshmi, Sarasvati, Rama, Siva, Kartikeya, Jaya, Vijaya, the Peacock, the Serpent, Hanuman, the lion, the buffalo, the demon, the ten avatars, the ten Mahavidyas, and indeed all the figures represented in the chals.

The principal bedstead is then offered to Durga, so is the canopy with the mulmantra and handsful of flowers. The Devi is then prayed.

THE PRAYER.

OM DURGA, thou art Siva, the Dispenser of Peace, thou art Brahmani, thou art beloved by Brahma, thou art the adored of all beings, I salute thee, well-wisher, for ever! Benefactor, beautifier, purifier, blameless, oh the best of all beauties, lady of the universe, mother of the universe, Chandika, I salute thee! Essence of all the gods, oh Devi, the defender of the universe, thou art adored by Brahma, Vishnu and Isa, for ever I bow to Uma. Oh Dweller on the Vindyas, Vindya-homed, oh resident of heavenly places, thou art yogini, oh mother of the yoginis, to thee I bow, oh Chandika, oh Devi, thou art the mother of Isvara, thou art Isvari and beloved of Isvara, I salute thee Durga for ever, thou crossing-boat in the ocean of life.

Then lie prostrate before the goddess and so lying recite as follows: Om I bow to Narayani, the fountain of all blessings heavenly and worldly, the fulfiller of all wishes, the adorable, the mother of the gods, oh! Gauri. Om destroyer of the buffalo, oh Mahamaya, Chamunda, skull-wreathed, grant me life, health, and wealth, I bow to thee. Oh save me from Bhutas, Pisachas and Pretas, oh Paramesvari, protect me for ever from gods, men, and beasts. Oh be gratified goddess Durga in the several forms of Uma, Brahmani Virgin, and Visvarupini. Om Fountain of Prosperity confer on me beauty, honor, reputation, good luck, child, wealth, indeed all that I wish. Oh! Durga, who hastbeen painted with chandan and anointed with saffron,and whose hands have been decorated with Vilva leaves, I have taken thy protection. Om thou art Bhagavati in times of fear, Katyayani when fulfilling our desires, Kausiki when gratifying us, oh Katyayani I bow to thee, oh Prachanda give me children for ever, oh well-pleased girl of the gods, oh Ugra give fame to the family and victory to me. Thou art Rudrachanda and Prachanda, the destroyer of the army of Prachanda, oh Devi, protect us everywhere, lady of the universe I bow to thee. Thou art Durga, because thou protectest us from danger, and because thou savest us from all evils, give us virtuous propensities and salvation, Devi for ever be gratified with me. Oh Durga, most powerful Durga, oh friend to the help-seeking, save me, oh subduer of the buffalo demon be pleased with me. Absolve me from sins, remove my miseries, save me from remorse and anxiety, from disease, from all causes for repentance, and ignorance, oh spouse of Siva. Om Kali, Kali, Mahakali, oh Kalika, destroyer of sins, oh dispenser of virtuous motives, I bow to thee, Narayani. Give victory in times of war, give wealth at home and virtuous motives and kindness, give me oh Devi I salute thee. Oh Kali give me life, oh Siva give me children for ever, oh Mahamaya give me wealth, oh Narasinhi give me honor. Om may Chandika guard my head, may Mahesvari guard my forehead, may Chamundi guard my eyes and may Parvati guard my hearing. Mahamaya guard my smelling, Hemavati guard my face, Amvica guard my tongue, Kalika guard my neck, Katyayani guard my shoulders, Siva guard my hands, Sambhupriya guard my arms, Parvati guard my breast, Varahi guard my waist,

Chandika guard my navel, Narasinhi guard my sides, Bhavani guard my back, Rudrani guard my bosom, Bhavani guard my thighs, Aparna guard the two thigh roots, Durga gaurd my legs, Srimati Sarvamangala gurd my all body, Vishalakshi guard my organs, and Chandika my teeth, Chamunda guard my heart, and Kalika guard all the parts.

Durga save me from blindness, from leprosy, from poverty, sickness, and most painful sorrow, and from cold relatives and friends, also from misfortunes. His is well established dominion and his is inexhaustible treasury, and his is true power, on whose head you dwell. I am praised, I have done, my life is successful when you oh Durga, have entered my house and accepted arghya, flower, and other offerings. Oh blessed Devi! bless me, Amen! Then seven times circumambulate the goddess.

THE HOMA.

After the sacrifice is over this ceremony is performed by a separate priest, sitting on the west of the Homa fire-pit, and annointing the place with cow-dung and drawing three lines from north to the south by kusa half a cubit long, and taking up by the thumb and the fourth finger the earth thus scraped out, he throws it towards north-east corner. He then sprinkles water over the place and from the fire brought from the right in a brazen pot takes a flaming fire-brand and recites. Om I snatch the flesh-eating Agni, and may this flame go to the regions of Yama with my enemies, and the priest throws the brand towards the south-west corner. He takes another brand and repeats—Om let Agni, mouth of all beings, carry the offered ghi to the Jatavedas and other gods, and he then places the same on the lines facing towards himself. Then naming Agni, the priest says, Om thou art Valada, come hither! Om thou art red-browed, red-bearded red-haired, hard-bodied, and red-bellied. Thou art seated on a goat. Agni, thou hast the sacerdotal thread and beads, thou art seven-flamed and spear-handed. Then with meditation the priest worships Agni with chandan and other offerings and says, Om Agni with feet and hands stretched every way, eyes penetrating every place, mouth placed above thy head, the universe thy form, I salute thee! He next places to the right of this fire some kusa grass with their nice blades towards the seat of Brahma, and with a Vedic hymn circumambulates the fire. Then with another hymn he draws by the left hand a kusa blade from the Homa kunda and throws it to the south-west corner with the following mantra. Om here I am sitting in the house of Vrhaspati, and I announce to Agni that the sun is begotten of gods, so also to Vayu and to Prithivi. So saying the Brahman who represents Brahma, with kussa in hand sits on the profferred kusas facing Agni. The priest then places near the hota the several articles of the Homa sacrifice, and after some mantras and signs commences ahuti.

The ahuti implies offering on the flame handsful of ghi with vilva-leaves in the name of Durga. Indeed, the ahutis are offered to Durga through Agni.

THE KUMARI PUJA(46) :—A Brahman girl younger than nine years is respectfully placed on a carpet and offerings of cosmetics and sweetmeats and ornaments and clothes are made to her.

In the evening the usual arati or lustration is performed and offerings of sweetmeats and fruits are given.

THE ASHTAMI PUJA.

HAVING finished the morning ceremonies with kusa in hand the priest performs the achaman, worships Narayana, establishes as stated before the ordinary arghya, and after purifying the carpet as before meditates Durga in the form described above.. Placing a flower on the head, the priest worships the goddess as before mentally. He next establishes the special arghya and annoints tbe reflection of the Devi in a mirror with the mantras and drugs mentioned above. Then worshipping Surya, Ganesa, and other gods as before he adores Brahma, Sarasvati, Lakshmi, Indra, the nine planets, and the Pitha. Meditating again Durga in her above described form he presents her several offerings and makes the goat sacrifice as before. On this day generally two goats are sacrificed and each is separately worshipped. Afterwards worshipping the nine Patricas and making the Japa the priest offers the same to the Goddess. He then prays as before.

Having worshipped Vishnu with sixteen offerings the priest presents the same to Ganesa and to all other gods figured on the chal or represented in the idols. He next makes seven circumambulations round the pratima, and worships the associate gods and goddesses. These are firstly the Matris(47) who are invoked and worshipped with several hymns respectively. The Ashta Nayikas(48) are then invoked and worshipped. The Batukas(49) are then invoked and worshipped. The sixty-four Yoginis are then invoked and worshipped. The Pithas(50) are next invoked and worshipped. Then follows the worship of the titular deities(51) of different countries. Then the Saktis(52) are invoked and worshipped; also the weapons(53) of the gods and goddesses, the Kshetrapalas(54) and the Dikpalas(55).

A square filled with party-coloured powders according to the Sastras(56) is made, and in it at prescribed places nine ghatas are established, and these are decorated with nine differently coloured flags. The eight Dikpalas are then invoked in the several ghatas and worshipped, and Brahma, Ananta and several other gods in the central one. The sixteen Matrikas are also invoked and worshipped. The usual Homa is made with the fire established on the previous day; but if it has not been kept up, a new fire has to be established The Kumari is also worshipped.

At noon of the Ashtami day after the sacrifices and other pujas have been performed a peculiar custom of the fumigation of frankincense is observed. The ladies of the house having offered handsful of flowers to the goddess, seat themselves on the court yard facing the idol and burn frankincense on their palms and heads. Small shallow earthen vessels called sharas and malshis are held on the palms and over head and flaming faggots are placed on them. The priests throw pounded aromatic resins on the flame, which blaze up with unusual brilliancy. Thrice the incense is put in each vessel and three sets of vessel are placed three times on the palms and the head of each lady. These flaming pans are offered to Durga. At the end of the ceremony a boy is placed on the lap of each lady who blesses him. During this ceremony the drums play a peculiar tune. At midnight of Ashtami the goddess is worshipped with sixteen kinds of offerings and the sacrifice and the homa are also made. This is the day when free-will offerings and offerings for the prosperity of each member of the family are made.

THE SANDHYA PUJA takes place at the conjunction of Ashtami and Navami tithis. The priest with kusa in hand and having as before made his achaman and having worshipped Narayana establishes as before an ordinary arghya and worships the Janitar gods. The vetalas being propitiated and the Bhuta and other suddhis and Nyasas being performed the priest with a flower on the head meditates on Chamunda as follows: Om terrific-faced Kali, holding a drawn sword and a noose and a (curious) club, wreathed with human skulls, dressed in elephant-skin, lean, emaciated and terrible, wide-mouthed, tongue dreadfully protruded, maddened, blood red-eyed, and filling the four quarters of the globe with hideous cries. He next worships her as before mentally, and establishing a special arghya scatters on his own person three handsful of flowers. He then worships Ganesa and other gods, and again meditating Durga strews flowers on her head with, Om the destroyer of the Daksha yajna &c. Om Hrim to Chamunda. He next worships her with sixteen offerings, makes the usual goat scarifice, dedicates a hundred and eight lamps, which are lighted at the time of lustration, and completes the puja with Homa and Kumari worship.

THE NAVAMI PUJA.

THIS is a repetition of the Ashtami Puja in all respects excepting that a greater number of goats, sheep, and buffalo are sacrificed together with a gourd and a bundle of sugarcane. On this day after the Homa is finished Agni is requested to retire so also the other gods and goddesses, and the priests receive their dakshina or fee. After the sacrifices have been offered the Great Arati is performed, and the members of the family bow prostrate before the goddess, and then the Vijaya, that is the ceremony of embracing each other and forgetting and forgiving of past offences, takes place. At the end of homa the head member of the family paints his forehead with the ashes of the homa fire.

Certain families celebrate the kadamati, as it is called, on the Navami day after the sacrifices are over. The principal members lie prostrate on the court-yard aud embracing each other sing the praise of Durga, with drums beating. Then in a large procession they enter the houses of such relatives and neighbours as have held the Puja, where these join with their drums &c., the united procession enters other houses, and the parties return the visit to each other by turn.

THE DASAMI PUJA.

THE priest having performed his morning ceremonies as usual, worships Narayana &c., and does the usual Nyasa &c. &c. He then bids farewell to the ghatas saying, Om pardon us, and then invokes Durga staying in the offered flowers(57) with the following, Om pure gold bright Devi residing in the flowers, I medidate thee, cheerful-faced goddess, the subduer of the vanity of Daityas and Danavas. He then scatters flowers abundantly on her. Having next drawn a circle on the north-east side, and placed the offered flowers within it, he worships the goddess with the mantra ' Om Chandesvari &c.," and presents The relics of offered victuals to the Chandalini devi in a prescribed form. He next makes the farewell address to the Devi. After placing a pot of water before her, and touching her seat with the hand says, Om rise oh Devi Chamunda after thou hast received this auspicious worship, and ordained my prosperity with the eight Saktis Om proceed now to thy appropriate place, the residence of the immutable deity, so that thou mayst have mercy on me, and mayst thou in thine ineffable goodness revisit this abode. Oh goddess, mother of all worlds, and adored by me, now depart to thy proper place, that thou mayst return to me after the lapse of a year. Oh mother Bhagavati and supreme goddess dost thou now retire, in order to revisit me, and dispel all my difficulties. Move on in the stream of water and dwell in thy home for my benefit. With these mantras move the pratima, and deposit the image of the goddess in the mirror in water. Om rise Devi Chamunda, thou hast had thy auspicious Puja &c., as above. Then raising the pratima with the Navapatrica, carry her to the bank of a running stream, " Om Devi dost thou dive into this water together with the prosperous Patricas. I deposit thee in water for the augmentation of my children, life, and wealth. Om Devi being worshipped depart, retire, to that best of places, thy abode, so that at the expiration of a year thou mayst recall hither.

In the afternoou at an auspicious moment the idol is brought down to the court-yard, where the ladies of the house, bedicked and bejewelled, assemble to perform certain parting ceremonies. They paint their feet with a red paint, and burdened in an interesting fashion with silver jugs, pots, and other auspicious(58) articles they describe some graceful curves with open palms, holding betel leaves in hand, and then offer to the idols well-spiced pounded betel leaves. The ladies then circumambulate the idols seven times, at the same time dropping water from a silver jug, and lastly a plate full of rice with silver, and gold coins, and fruits is thrown over the heads of the idols. This part of the ceremony is performed by the head male member of the family passing the plate and the head female member receiving the same in her clothes, all the while the drums beat a peculiar tune.

After this the idol is taken without the house and carefully tied on a frame of bamboos and carried on the shoulders of bearers to the river side with great pomp, drums beating, fools dancing antics, all kinds of music playing, flags flying &c. The idol is then taken on a couple of boats and after cruising a little is thrown overboard with the following mantra. Om this worship, my goddess is complete to the best of my power, for my protection wast thou invoked, now hie thee to thy best home. The Pratima is then consigned to the river, after which follow a variety of sports and auspicious rites with beating of drums, and loud clamours, together with blowings of conch-shells, transports, and percussions of mrndagas, patahas and all sorts of drum instruments; and throwing of dust and mud, and pastimes, frolics, and other pantomimic games. The parties return home, chanting the prayer to the Devi described above, and the drums and flutes playing "when again shall the goddess return, oh where is the goddess gone!" After the idol has been deposited in the river the members of the family assemble with relatives and friends, and from the bank let loose a Coraccias indica(59), then all return home in procession, a Brahmin carrying one of the ghatas on the head.

All the members of the family assemble in the hall of worship, which is dimly lighted compared with the brilliant illumination of the previous three nights. The whole scene is solemn. The head of the family writes upon a bit of plantain or vela leaf the name of Durga, and is followed by the other members by turn. The priest sprinkles holy water upon the party assembled with the mantras commencing with "Om surastham-abhishin-chantu &c.," recited at the bathing of the Navapatrica on the Saptami Day—

SANTIH! SANTIH! SANTIH! HARI OM!

with the brilliant [illegible] of the precious [illegible] angels. The [illegible] is solemn. For instance the Family writes upon a bit of blanket [illegible] the name of [illegible], and [illegible] by the other inmates in turn. The [illegible] [illegible] [illegible] [illegible] [illegible] with the [illegible] [illegible] [illegible] [illegible] [illegible] [illegible] the [illegible] of the [illegible] on the [illegible] Day.

[illegible] [illegible] [illegible] [illegible] O [illegible]

APPENDIX.

NOTES.

(1.) The size of the pratima varies greatly in different families. Some have the plank about $4\frac{1}{3}$ cubits long, and the figures are accordingly about 4 cubits high. Such enormously large and unwieldy pratimas are rare. In the Sastras, however, there is no direction given as to the size of the pratima, except when it is made of precious metals or crystals, though it is expressly stated that the pratima should be so made as to excite veneration and love. Miniature pratimas may be here and there seen, but they are not general. The usual size of the pratima is with plank about $3\frac{1}{4}$ cubits long and $1\frac{1}{2}$ cubits broad, these dimensions are observed every year in the construction of the same. Some families have pratimas made of metals, a composition of copper, silver, zinc and other metals, is preferred, copper predominating. Such pratimas are permanent, and are not thrown away on the tenth day of the moon. In such cases a ghata is usually established on the occasion of the Durga Festival, which after the puja is over is deposited in water. Those, who have other murtis or representations such as Sinha-Vahini (the-ten armed goddess standing on a lion and the asura), Jagaddhatri (the four-armed goddess seated on a lion), Annapurna (the two-armed goddess distributing rice and other food) or other figures of Durga Sakti, establish the Navapatrica and the usual ghatas. The ghata and the Navapatrica are thrown into the river after the completion of the puja.

A marked conservatism rules the whole ceremony, the same forms and dimensions of the idols are observed from year to year, the same man or his heir moulds, paints, or decorates, the same priest or his representative officiates in worship, even the same parties who supply the furnitures, the edibles, the perfumes &c. &c., are engaged as the festival comes round each year.

At places situate far from rivers the idols are deposited in some large tanks in the village, and such tanks are always protected for that purpose. The Sastras, however enjoin that the idol should be carried on a boat or on the shoulders of men and immersed in a stream with sports, frolics, and loud cheers.

The bodhana for Durga Puja may be as stated in the text commenced on the ninth day of the dark fortnight preceding the month of Asvina. Should the navami be distributed over two civil days, that portion of it is to be preferred, which has the Ardra asterism, for, the Sastras say, in the month of Isa, dark fort-night in the navami tithi when the moon is in Ardra asterism (*a* Orionis) the goddess is aroused on the Vel tree. But some are of opinion that as the word bodhana (arousing) is used, the ceremony ought to be celebrated at night, and not during the day, but Raghunandana says that by the phrases (untimely) and " bodhana" (arousing)—Dakshinanayana or the Southern progress of the sun is meant, which is the night of the gods, *i. e.*, the Autumnal festival as distinguished from the Vernal when also the goddess Durga is worshipped, the Vernal festival being known as Vasanti Puja.

In the performance of the autumnal ceremony preference is given to forenoon, for, the Sastras say, the Devi is to be invoked, welcomed in, worshipped, and farewelled in the morning, and therefore that portion of the navami in conjunction with Ardra is to be preferred which falls in the forenoon, but if the conjunction takes place later, the bodhana should be performed before sunset. In the Jyotisharnava it is stated that commencing from the lagna of Kanya (Virgo) to that of Mina (Pisches) whenever the asterism Ardra is in conjunction with navami, the bodhana is to be performed at that very moment. In the month of Asvina the sun rises in the sign Virgo and sets in the seventh sign from it, hence the day is implied by the above quoted passage. In case, however, the conjunction of navami should take place on the forenoons of both days, that portion of navami which falls on the second is considered most auspicious. But on no account whatever the forenoon should be departed from, even should there be no conjunction of the asterism Ardra; for the conjunction of the same is not deemed absolutely necessary though desirable. In the Sankalpa for the bodhana the conjunction of the asterism is mentioned, and when it is absent, objection may be made to the mantra as inapplicable, but the inappropriateness is cured by the repetition of the word Om.

On the sixth day also the bodhana of the Goddess may be performed, but then in the bodhana mantra "on the evening of the sixth I arouse thee" is to be added. In case the Shashthi falls on both days the bodhana is to be performed on that day, on the evening of which the Shashthi tithi falls, inasmuch as it is an evening ceremony, and the inviting of the Goddess being quite a different ceremony may be performed on the evening of the following day, when there is no Shashthi, *i. e.* the evening preceding the Saptami Puja. But the Shashthi being in the evening of both days, the last day is to be preferred for bodhana, and the inviting is also to be performed on that evening. The Sastras say the learned are to invite on the previous evening the sacrificial gods who are to be worshipped on the following day. In the absence of both the Jyeshtha asterism, (*a*, *r*, *t*. Scorpionis) which is auspicious for inviting, and the Shashthi tithi, the invitation of the Gods should take place on the evening preceding the Saptami Puja. In the Brahmanda Nandikesvara Purana "the worshipper should invite the Goddess Chandica residing in the Vel tree on the evening preceding the day of the entrance of the Navapatrica." It needs however be remembered that the excess of a tithi over sixty dandas is not recognised in the performance of any ceremony except in the observance of ekadasi.

The Saptami Puja is initiated with the introduction of the Navapatrica, which should be observed in the morning. "The introduction of the Navapatrica is," say the Sastras "to be observed in the Saptami tithi in conjunction with the asterism Mula (*l, n, x, i, s, m, e.* Scorpionis") when the asterism is not available in the morning the entrance is to be made in Saptami without it, for in the performance of the autumnal worship of Durga from the entrance of the Navapatrica to the depositing of the idol in water, the rising of the sun is to be observed, and not the conjunction of the tithi with the asterism."

The Jyotish says, "the entrance of the Navapatrica in the morning is attended with prosperity and success; it gives also health, wealth, and victory, but the entrance of the same at noon is productive of distress and pestilence and of destructive war among mankind; the same if performed in the evening leads to imprisonment, slaughter, civil war, and destructions by snake-bites. If on account of Mula asterism one observes the Navapatrica entrance after sunset, he brings destruction on his sovereign with seven departments of his State, and on the peace of the world. Therefore let princes introduce Navapatrica at the auspicious dawn of Saptami even avoiding the Mula asterism for the good of their people."

The Ashtami Puja should be similarly observed in the forenoon. The Sastras say for the sake of barabela (the daily inauspicious moments) the worship of

Durga should not be delayed. The Sandhi Puja should be commenced twenty-four minutes preceeding the conjunction of theAshtami and Navami tithis, and the animal sacrifice pertaining to this Puja should be offered just at the occurrence of the conjunction. The Puja may be commenced a little later, but on no account the scarifice should be made during Ashtami.

The Visarjana of the Goddess should be held on the morning of the Dasami with Sravana asterism (*a*, *b*, *c*, Aquilœ). The Vrhannandikesvara Purana says, from the entrance of Bhagavati to the Visarjana, all the ceremonies are to be performed by the learned at dawn with prescribed lunations, and the Linga Purana says, the worship of Durga should be performed at dawn even without the conjunction of the asterisms. The Bhavishya Purana says, the devotee should worship the Goddess for three days from the Saptami, or for two or four days according to the decrease or increase of the tithis. The Linga Purana, however, says, Indra is to be deposited in water on the eighth day of worship and Parvati (Durga) on the fourth, a departure from this rule shall be visited with the destruction of the sovereign, the empire, and wealth. The increase of either of the tithis (lunations) Ashtami or Navami may cause a portion of the Dasami tithi to fall on the fifth civil day from the Saptami, and as the Visarjana of the Goddess is to be performed on the morning when Dasami is available, the question arises whether the Goddess is to be retained for four days in the house. Similarly on the decrease of any of the tithis the first day may be a tryahasparsa (three tithis falling on the same civil day) and on the fourth day from Saptami no fraction of Dasami may be present. Raghunandana holds that under such circumstances the Goddess is to be worshipped for four days or for two days as the case may be, that is,if the increase of the tithis necessitate the worship for four days it is to be thus observed, Saptami Puja on the first, Ashtami on the second, Sandhi Puja on the third, and Navami Puja on the fourth ; similarly on the decrease of the tithis, the worship is to be performed for two days, Saptami Puja on the first and Ashtami Puja, Sandhi Puja, and Navami Puja on the second.

It may be here noted that in the celebration of the autumnal festival the secondary (Gauna) lunar month is counted *i. e.*, the month from full moon to full moon and not from new moon to new moon.

If after the sankalpa for puja has been made the yajamana becomes impure by reason of the death of some member of the family or by some new birth in it the puja is not to be stopped, for Yajnavalkya says : In vrata, yajna, marriage, funeral ceremony, homa, worship, and japa the impurity does not interefere, if the same should have been commenced. The appointment of the priest is said to be commencement of a yajna, (sacrifice), the sankalpa that of vrata and japa, the nandi ceremony that of marriage and the preparation of rice that of a Sradha or funeral ceremony. But the Durgotsava being considered a Nitya ceremony, the yajamana's impurity, even if it occurs before the sankalpa is made does not interfere with its performance, the family priest or the spiritual guide in that event making the sankalpa for the yajamana.

The Rudra Yamala Tantra gives several directions, as to the form, materials &c., of the pratima. The vedi or the pavement is to be made of earth upon which is to be described a mandala, and in the centre of this mandala or a circular mystic figure is to be placed an earthen jar filled with water, over which the representation of the Devi is set up. But this cannot be done with heavy and big idols of clay as they are now made in Bengal. The Devi Purana says, the representation (pratima) is to be made of gold or of other precious metals or a picture of the

Goddess may be used as a substitute for the idol. The Kalika Purana says, the Devi may be worshipped in the Siva linga or in mystic circles, or in a book, or in fire, or in idols, or in painting, or in an arrow, or in a sword, or in water, or in written characters &c. The Devi Purana adds the trident as an article on which the Devi may be worshipped.

According to Hayasirshapancharatra the idol may be made of earth, wood, iron, crystals, stones, fragrant substances and flowers. The worship of the Goddess in wooden figure fulfils all the wishes of the worshipper, in gold gives him salvation, in silver heavenly bliss, in copper longevity, in bell-metal peace, in sand victory, in marble, enjoyment, in crystal beatitude, and in clay all put together.

The pratima if made of any material other than clay should be constructed in the house of the worshipper and should not exceed a cubit in height.

The pratima should never be made of burnt clay, for the Krtyatatvarnava says, one who worships the goddess Durga in burnt clay is converted into ashes by the wrath of the goddess. Lime should not be used in the construction of the idol, though in cases of Brahmans the Sastras permit the use of white earth (not lime) and of Kshatriyas red earth. Inordinately big idols are held to lead to revolutions, defective idols to the destruction of the architect, lean-bellied idols to the production of famine, thin-made idols of poverty, scarred idols of the disease of fistula, weaponless idols of death, the blunt nosed goddess of depression of spirits, and low-breasted of the destruction of one's friends. The hall in which the goddess is to be worshipped should be quadrangular, regular, secluded, decorated with svastica and other auspicious articles, beautifully canopied and screened. The table is to be placed on a Vedi four cubits long and to be covered with carpets of silk, wool and skin.

The Bhavishya Purana says the paint should be of

white earth and the figures described of various weapons and yantras. The ground rice is evidently a substitute of white clay (chalk) mentioned in the Sastras.

(2.) THE mock ornaments are made of the pith of sola, the Indian cork, and the corks are cut into thin sheets and required designs by men of the mali (gardener) caste, whose business it also is to prepare garlands and ornaments of flowers and of mock flowers (of sola). Formerly the malis used to decorate the idols. But now-a-days the ornamentation the idols is very expensive and forms a lucrative trade by itself, and those, who follow it, are called Sajwallas (ornament-makers) or Dak-wallas (dealers in tin.) The crude materials used in preparing mock-ornaments are sheets of sola, foils of tin beat into a variety of patterns, plates of mica slates split into the thinnest sheets, possible and one side silvered over with mercury, beads of various size and patterns of sola or some light wood wound round with silver or gold laces and little discs of gold or silver. These are combined into a variety of shapes and forms and made to represent the jwelled ornaments used by the ladies of Bengal.

The head dress is called a Mukuta, it is a peculiarly shaped, flat ornament a few inches broad, wound round the forehead, a disc like projection, rising high from the central portion of the same. The entire ornament is made of iron wires twisted and curved into a cluster of graceful flowers and leaves. This ornament has no equivalent in the boudoir of the Bengali lady. It is exclusively used in decorating idols, it is something like a tiara.

The hairs of the idols are made of blackened jute. A common pratima if ordinarily decorated costs generally between Rs. 80 to Rs. 100, but the actual cost of richly ornamented idols sometimes exceeds five times that sum.

(3.) THE worshipping of the four figures on both sides of Durga is not mentioned in the Sastras, though the custom of constructing and worshipping them separately is pretty general. In the Autumnal Durga Puja the only deities to be worshipped are the Devi, the lion and the demon. Raghunandana in his Durgotsava tatva, a part of his elaborate work entitled Tithi-tatva, does not even notice the four idols nor do the several Puranas, which treat of Durgotsava, make mention of the worship of Lakshmi, Sarasvati, Kartikeya and Ganesa. The popular belief is that the above four deities are the children of Parvati the daughter of Himavat. Indeed this idea is preserved in the popular songs sung on the occasion of the autumnal festival. The Devi is supposed to have come to the house of Himavat with her children about this time of the year and Menaka the wife of Himavat is represented in several Yatras (operas) as urging on Himavat to invite Gauri to her house.

Lakshmi and Sarasvati, however, are described in the Puranas as Saktis equal in rank to Durga, Kartikeya alone is the son of Parvati.

Jayasinha in his celebrated compilation entitled the Kalpadruma says that as no abhisheka or bathing can be held of clay or painted figures, the same should be performed either on a shining sword, on a speculum mirror, or on five jars of water, four of which are to be placed in the four corners of the hall. The Kalika Purana adds, on these five jars of water invoke and worship the goddess Kaushiki with her four associates viz. the Sun, Agni, Isana, and Vishnu. "The Gaudiyas (Bengalis)," says Jayasinha, "worship the goddess Durga with four associate gods viz. Ganesa, who is the substitute of Agni according to the Sivarchana Chandrica, Kartikeya who is Ganesa's self, and Siva, Vishnu and the sun, because the Gaudiyas do not make a separate worship of Agni."

The Tantras however descirbe Ganesa, Kartikeya, Sarasvati and Lakshmi as children of Durga but nowhere it is stated that they should be worshipped together with Durga in the autumnal festival. The Brhaddharma Purana, it is said, has enjoined the construction of the idols of the above four with that of Durga in the autumnal festival, but as no M.S. of the same is accessible, this statement may be verified by these who possess the original.

(4.) THE chals or top-pieces are nowhere mentioned in the Sastras. It is not known how these and the four superfluous idols mentioned above, have been associated with Durga in the autumnal representation, and when and by whom these innovations were made. A tradition is extant that Raja Krshnachandra of Krshnanagara in Navadvipa first worshipped the goddess in clay figures described above. How far it is correct I cannot say. The allusion of the worship of the quintuple figure by the Bengalis in Jayasinha's Kalpadruma, however, throws much doubt on the above tradition. Jayasinha lived in the days of Aurungzebe long before Raja Krshnachandra of Navadvipa flourished. The older form of the autumnal groups consists of the Devi, her lion, and asura it may still be seen worshipped in several orthodox families.

The Mahavidyas are the female incarnations of the Deity. They are described in the Tantras to be ten in number. They are the several extraordinary mani. festations of (Sakti) Force incarnated on extraordinary occasions. Like the ten incarnations (Avataras) of Vishnu they came forth at times when the divine interference was necessary for the protection of the world.

To express the idea in the words of Leibnitz's charge to the Princess of Wales put forth in his celebrated letter, "Sir Isaac Newton and his followers have also a very odd opinion concerning the work of God. According to their doctrine God Almighty wants to wind up His watch from time to time; otherwise it would cease to move. He had not, it seems, sufficient foresight to make it a perpetual motion. Nay the machine of God's making is so imperfect, according to these gentlemen, that He is obliged to clean it now and then by an extraordinary concourse, and to mend it as a clock-maker mends his work." The ten Avataras (incarnations) of Vishnu, the Deity in the male form, appeared similarly on ten extraordinary occasions, which are summed up by Jayadeva in his prayer to the ten Avataras in the following words: To recover the lost Vedas, to sustain the world, to raise the universe, to punish the daityas, to mislead Bali, to annihilate the kshatriyas, to subdue Ravana, to ply the plough, to protect the meek, and to destroy the mlechchhas.

The above are the objects for which the ten avataras of Vishnu were manifested. The avataras are the Matsya the fish incarnation; the Kachchha or the tortoise incarnation (Colosochelys atlas?), the Varaha the boar incarnation, the Nrsinha, the half lion and the half man incarnation, the Vamana the dwarf incarnation, the incarnation in the person of Parasurama, the son of Jamadagni, who several times annihilated the Kshatriya race; the same in that of Rama the well-known hero of the Ramayana, ditto in that of Valarama, the contemporary and cousin of Krshna, whose weapon was the plough; ditto in that of Buddha who inculcated the doctrine of treating every animate being with kindness and lastly Kalki, the terrible incarnation, which is to destroy the un-sacrificing heretics and unbelievers. The Tantras have for each of the above mentioned Pauranic ten avataras (male incarnations of the Deity) one female incarnation (Mahavidya.) They are as follows: Kali is the force of Krshna, Tara that of Rama, Vagala that of the Kachchha, Dhumavati that of the Fish, Chhinnamasta that of Nrsinha, Bhairavi that of Varaha, Sundari that of Parusarama, Bhuvanesvari that of Vamana, Kamala that of Budha and Durga that of Kalki. In the above enumeration of the ten Mahavidyas occur some new names but no two Tantras agree on this point. The above is taken from the Mundamala Tantra.

The Yoginis, Batukas, and such other abstract manifestations are multiplied without number in the Tantras and they occupy a prominent place in the same. The modes of worshipping them and the yantras or mystic figures peculiar to each with the exact forms and peculiar vijas or roots with mula mantras are the principal topics of the Tantras. Several chapters are devoted to the kinds of places suited for the worship of each and the names of trees sacred to each and the days of the year allotted to the worship of each.

(5.) THE practice of not presenting edibles to the Goddess during the day observed by the Chaudhuris of Makardah is singular and needs some explanation. It is said that on the occasion of the Puja one year the head of the family was imprisoned by the Nawab of Murshidabad, after the Navami bodhana had commenced. The goods and chattels of the Chaudhuri being confiscated, the family was reduced to the greatest penury, the more so because no neighbour or friend dared openly offer any assistance to a family interdicted by the Nawab. But as the Navami bodhana had been commenced the priest called daily and offered flowers, vel-leaves, and water to the goddess and recited the Devimahatmya.

According to custom the idol was ready for worship on the evening of the Shashthi and as the family had nothing in this world to offer, a consultation was held with the priest for the disposal of the idol. The priest advised that the usual establishment of the Navapatrica should be made and the idols worshipped with flowers and water if nothing else was available. Accordingly the usual anointing of the Navapatrica was made, and the worship of the goddess performed with flowers and water. On the evening of the Saptami however the head of the family being released returned home and being told on enquiry how the worship had been performed, directed that rice be boiled immediately and offered to the goddess on plantain leaves as no plates were available. The goddess was accordingly worshipped in the night with boiled rice. The year succeeding the puja the family was blessed with prosperity and when the festival returned the head of the family insisted on offering boiled rice to the goddess on plantain leaves, saying that as this practice had brought him prosperity he should adhere to it all his life. His descendants observe the same practice to this day. The Mukuryas of Halisahar, it is said do not worship the goddess during the day nor do they observe the Sandhi Puja. Instances of such family peculiarities may be multiplied without end.

(6.) Oleo-resin of Diptocarpus turbinatus.

(7.) The mystic figures are numerous, each goddess has a separate figure for her. The Yantras as they are called are considered the symbols of the goddesses, and on them the Saktis or the female manifestations are worshipped. Most of the Yantras are combinations of triangular figures placed either in centres or petals of the lotuses, some are like the Freemason's inverted triangles placed one in each petal of a painted lotus, and the vija or the root, or the mula mantra of the goddess inscribed the required number of times on each petal.

(8.) The kalpa literally means the will or the resolution to perform a ceremony, and in the Durgotsava, the usual kalpa is that which commence, from the first tithi (lunation) immediately following the new moon of Asvina; the Navaratri festival therefore commences on the first lunation after the new moon and ends on the dasami or tenth lunation. This festival, which is identical with the Durgotsava, may extend over ten or eight days according to the number of civil days equivalent to the nine lunations.

The Krtyakalpalata says that in the month of Asvina the Navaratri ought to be observed commencing from the pratipada till the navami. Or the triratra is to be observed from the saptami to the end of the navami.

The Durgabhaktitarangini says, that the kalpa may be of the following kinds viz., commencing from the dark navami, commencing from the bright pratipada (first lunation after the new moon), commencing from the sixth lunation (shashthi), commencing from the seventh (saptami) lunation or commencing from the eighth (ashtami) lunation, or the ninth (navami) lunation. And this authority divides the Bodhana into two kinds, the first on the dark navami intended for the arousing of the eighteen-armed goddess, and the second on the shashthi for that of the ten armed goddess. The Kalika Purana however says that at the bodhana the Demon and the Lion are to be worshipped as they are below the feet of the goddess, the navami bodhana is said to be only for the eighteen-armed goddess, and as the last named goddess has no demon under her feet at the navami bodhana, the ten armed goddess may also be aroused. The eighteen armed goddess is Chandi, she rests on a lion.

The Bhavishya Purana says that on the pratipada tithi cosmetics, pomades, and hair oils are to be offered to the Goddess. They are the mathaghasa, consisting of several aromatic drugs sold in the bazar under that name. These are fried and powdered and with the compound powder, the head is well rubbed before bathing. The same drugs are also used in perfuming palm oil for the hair, and the pomade made with wax, perfumed oils and otto.

On the second day (Dvitiya) silk threads and ribbons are to be offered for tying the locks of hair. On the third day (tritya) a mirror and vermillion and alaktaka are to be given to the goddess. Ordinarily a silvered looking-glass is offered as a mirror, but the scrupulous offer in addition to that a speculum mirror called the Darpan. The subjoined figure is that of a Darpan;

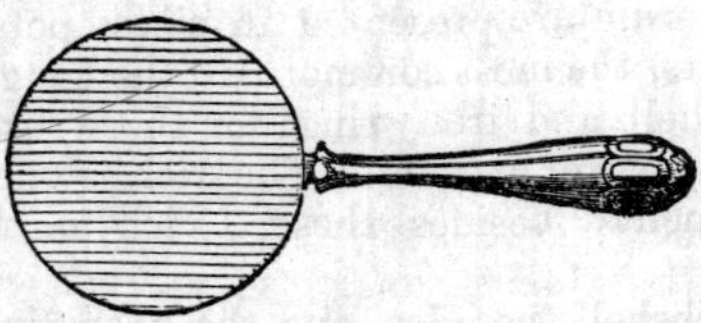

DARPAN.

The Darpan is made either of silver, steel, brass or the speculum metal in which silver predominates. A darpan is also used for bathing the idol or in other words whenever the Sastras enjoin the gods to be anointed the reflexion of the idols in the darpan is bathed. The darpan alone is immersed in a pot of water on the morning of Dasami when the Gods are bade farewell.

The Alaktaka is a chapeti or thin wadding of cotton dipped in tincture of lacdye. With it the soles of the feet are painted red and protected from being chaffed. In painting the feet it is soaked in water and being squeezed yields a red infusion. The alaktaka as well as the vermillion with which the portion of the forehead between the eye-brows is painted red are considered auspicious articles, and married women are alone permitted to use them. Their use is said to contribute to the longevity of the husband. The widows altogether refrain from both.

A tilaka is a gold head-dress, it is an oval convex piece of gold generally worn by Hindustani ladies on their forehead between the eye-brows. The eyes of gold are ancient ornaments,shaped like the eyes with a hole in the centre ; they are now put on stone idols to represent the eyes. On the fifth day (Panchami) are to be presented to the Devi chandana (unguents of sandal) and other beautifiers of the body such as perfumed oil, the misi (a paint for the teeth), virmillion, the henna, and unguent of kumkum (Croccus sativus) together with several ornaments. Chandana, perfumed oil, and kumkum are presented in silver pots, and as for ornaments, the most common are the bangles sawed from conchshell and iron ring for the wrist, covered over with a wire of gold. The rich alone present other ornaments besides these, such as bracelets, necklaces &c.

The conchshell bangles and the iron ring for the wrist are indispensable articles. They are considered auspicious and are supposed to give longevity to husbands. These together with the virmillion paint are the signs of a married lady.

The Matsya Purana says that from the pratipada tithi every day Brahma, Agni, Surya, Indra and other gods and Dikpalas are to be worshipped with at least five kinds of offerings. It adds that the Yajnas are fraught with danger, because the kingdom is destroyed if the proper articles are not offered in the Yajnas ; the priests suffer death if the mantras are not properly recited and applied, and the soul of the worshipper suffers damnation if the proper fees are not given to the priests.

(9.) THE Sastras say that no one is entitled to perform any ceremony unless he has observed the preliminaries, and therefore before the performance of any ceremony the daily morning rites must be performed. These are numerous, to wit early rising from bed, making obeisance to the earth and Narayana, repeating the names of several pious kings, and heroes, making obeisance to the several Nagas, washing oneself and performing the Dawn Sandhya and Ahnika. The Sandhya consists of the usual Achaman, washing the face and the limbs, the marjan or the rubbing of the body with a view to its purification, and the invoking and worshipping of the Savitri mantra. Then follows the Tantric Sandhya or the worshipping of the particular form of Sakti in the particular vija or root of the Goddess taught by the mantra-guru. It may be noticed that the last mentioned Sandhya is of later date. It has been introduced within the last three hundred years, and it is not in vogue in any other part of India than Bengal, and even here several Brahman families have no other mantra, and do not acknowledge any other spiritual guide than the Savitri-guru.

After the performance of the above-mentioned rites the worshipper should offer balis, and perform five homas for the expiation of the five-fold sin generated daily by the sweeping of the rooms, the lighting of the hearth, the grinding of the culinary spices, and such other unavoidable domestic duties. The balis are five-fold, consisting of the tarpans or oblations to the manes of the departed, of the offering to the gods of ghi upon fire, of the offering of food to Brahmans or guests, of the presentation of food to the domestic animals and birds such as the dogs and the crows, and of feeding one's self and family.

These are the daily morning duties of every religious man, and unless they are performed he is not at liberty to attend to his other vocations. The ceremonies following the daily dawn Sandhya may be performed any time before dinner, bnt it ought not to be taken until the guests have been fed and satisfied. But after the Sandhya has been performed, one is at liberty to officiate in any sacrifice or yajna. The priests should therefore perform the Sandhya at least, before he commences to worship Durga.

Kusa is Poa cynosuroides, Retz. It is a necessary article for every Hindu ceremony. No religious ceremony can be performed unless one holds kusa grass in hand. Indeed, the Sastras say, that all offerings whether to the gods or to the manes of the departed ought to pass over kusa, and therefore rings made of kusa are worn on occasions of religious ceremonies. When water has to be sprinkled over anything it is done with three blades of kusa tied in a peculiar manner called the tripatra. In the ceremonies to the manes almost every offering is to be accompanied with a mukuta (crest) made of kusa. In offering pieces of threads with the cake to the manes, the same are tied on a mukuta of kusa. Kusa is indispensable in ceremonies, but married women use the durva grass instead of kusa.

The collection of kusa for certain ceremonies is attended with much eclat. There are special moments fixed for the collection of the same. Kusa that has been collected during the southern progress of the sun cannot be used in any ceremony performed during the northern progress of the same. During the Dakshinayana collected-kusa retains its purity for eight days, but if kusa be collected during the northern progress of the sun (Uttarayana) it may be used in any ceremony during the year.

The Taittiriya Brahman of the Black Yajurveda devotes an entire section to the mantras &c. for collecting kusa grass. Many of those mantras are still in use in the collection of Kusa. The instrument for cutting the grass according to the Vedas ought to be made of the rib of a horse or a cow. The modern authors, however, have substituted it by an iron knife. The instrument is purified by a mantra and warmed on fire. A mantra has to be recited while cutting the grass, and with another mantra, invoking Pushan, the grass is to be tied in a bundle and borne on head to the sacrificial hall. Kusa grass is, however, rare in this part of Bengal, and the substitute generally used for it is kasa (Saccharum spontaneum). The Sastras say that durva, ulu, kasa, and sama-grass may be used as substitute if kusa be not available.

(10.) Achamana is the act of purifying one's body by thrice sipping water and touching several parts of the body with it. It should be performed before every ceremony. In performing it the palm is contracted, and the thumb placed behind the fore-finger and the other fingers kept straight, describing a cow's ear; a small quantity of water just sufficient to dip a masa is taken and thrice it is drunk, so that the water so drunk may reach the region of the heart. It is performed with the face towards the east, indeed almost all Daiva rites are performed with the face towards the east. Then the lips are touched with the tips of the fingers, with the thumb curved under the forefinger, the nose with the thumb and the ring-finger, the eyes and ears are touched each thrice, the navel with the little finger and the heart with the palm, and the head with the fingers put together and the roots of the arms with the tops of fingers. In the case of Kshatriyas the water drunk should be in such quantity as to touch the throat, and of Vaishyas to touch the mouth,but the Sudras should never drink it, but simply sprinkle it into the mouth. The achamana is accompanied by reciting Om Vishnu and the achamana Sukta "Om the Vishnu &c.", but the Sudras only repeat, Obeisance to Vishnu. The pranava Om should never be repeated by Sudras so also the phrases Svaha, Phat, Vashat, Voushat, and the several roots given in the text.

The symbolical achamana should be preceded by actual washing of the hands, the feet, and the face. Though according to the Sastras every thing done symbolically is equivalent to the actual performance of the same, the real performance of such ablutions and other actions, which are practicable, and can be performed without inconveniencing the worshipper, is insisted. Thus where water for the complete ablution of one's person is available, and when the individual can without injuring his health take a bath, such is ordained to be done. In deserts or places where water is scarce or not available, the mere gesticulation and the supposition of performing the achamana with water are quite sufficient. If after having performed the necessary achamana one has commenced a ceremony, and if he is interrupted by somebody the Sastras enjoin that a fresh achamana should be made. But in so doing he is not required to wash his hands and feet &c. again, nor to perform the several gesticulations noted above, the mere remembering of Vishnu is quite sufficient. Indeed, the entire performance appears to be a step towards the composing of ones self. The concentration of one's attention upon the object of worship or ceremony is only what is aimed at by the Sastras ; the Tantras equally in calculate the same principle. The authors of the Tantras attach so much importance to the externals of worship that they lose sight of the primary in the secondary object.

In the Taittiriya Brhmana of the B. Yajur Veda a separate mantra for achamana is given, which is however applicable to all sacrifices. The mantra is—Om the gods who know the ins and outs of sacrifice, enter this yajna with the Almighty God, the guardian of our mind, from the region of mind and let the sacrifice go on without hinderance.

---

(11) THE Brahman Sasana literally means the edict or commandment of Brahma the Creator. According to the Sastras every ceremony should be preceded by a Sankalpa or solemn resolution to perform the same, and while performing the ceremony, certain witnesses should be summoned to attest the same. This idea is of ancient origin, and may be traced so far back as the Ramayana, according to one recension of which Ramachandra and Sita are said to have offered cakes made of sand to the manes of Dasaratha. But subsequently on being questioned as to the truth of their statement of having performed the Sraddha they referred to the religious Fig tree and the river Phalgu who had seen the performance of the ceremony. Phalgu deposed differently and she was therefore cursed, and from that day the river Phalgu has been shallow. To the present day after performing the Sraddha obeisance, is made to Surya, the witness of all deeds. The names mentioned in the text as those of the witnesses appointed by Brahma are the names of such gods or existences as are present everywhere and at every time. They alone are competent to attest all actions done under the sun.

---

(12) THE udumvara literally means any thing made of the wood of the sacrificial fig tree or of copper, for udumvara is the name of the tree (Ficus

glomerata, Rox, and of the metal cruprum. Three vessels are necessary for the performance of a worship *viz.* the Prokshanipatra, a vessel from which water is sprinkled on the offerings, the Arghya patra or the vessel on which the argya is established, and the Sruva or a vessel to pour water or other liquids from; the Kosa with its two necessary appendages, the kusi and the kunda, serves the purpose of all the above mentioned three vessels together with the vessel for placing the Gods or their representations in the mirror while bathing them. The drawing annexed is that of a kosa:

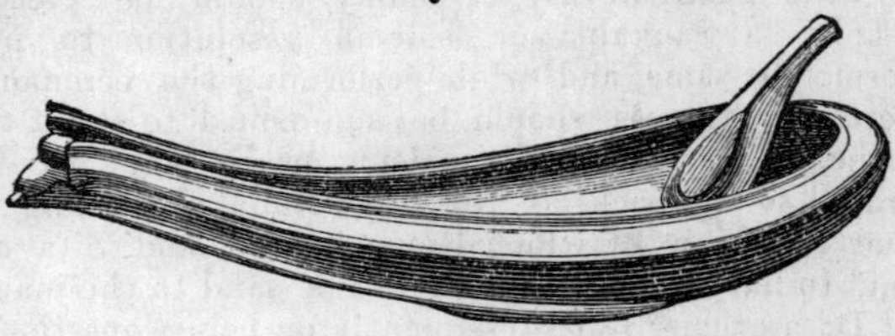

KOSA.

The smaller drawing is that of a kusi, a smaller kosa, and the circular dish is a kunda in which water offered to the Gods is put:

KUNDA.

The above three are the most necessary articles in religious ceremonies, for they are applicable to all purposes. The small kusi serves as the ladle to pour water with, it is a substitute of the Sruva, the kosa serves as a vessel for establishing the special arghya, the turned-out lip of the vessel holding the several articles of an arghya.

(13) THE Sankalpa as stated before is the solemn resolution for performing any thing religious. It is an indispensable preliminary as no ceremony, nay not even the ordinary gift should be made without it. A ceremony or any religious act is considered void without a Sankalpa. The reason is obvious. The Sastras enjoin the conscious performance of every ceremony. Any thing done unknowingly is not done according to the Sastras. Nay even such meritorious actions as entertaining a guest or feeding the hungry are not recognised if they are not performed with a Sankalpa. If the actual performance of any act is interrupted or put a stop to by any unforeseen event the Sankalpa or the necessary preparations for the same are quite sufficient. Thus, the principal part of a Sraddha, a ceremony to the manes of the departed, is the offering of the pinda (the cakes, made of the refuse of rice but if the Brahman should eat up the whole dish the pinda is still to be considered as offered. The Sapindana being a ceremony of mixing the pinda offered to the manes of the last departed with those offered to the earlier departed, the Sastras direct that fresh eatables are to be collected and the pinda offered with the same. An involuntary action is no action according to the Sastras. Similarly when a dying person is carried to the river-side, it is enjoined that he should be conscious of his presence there, otherwise the merit of such removal does not accrue to him. The Bhavishya Purana says, "O Prince whatever men perform without a Sankalpa, the meritorious effect of the act is diminished and a moiety of it is destroyed altogether." In the Brahma Purana the Sankalpa (vow) is made mentally, the abhilap (declaration of a vow) is made by words, and the upapadana (accomplishment of the same) by actual performance. The Sankalpa should be made with a vessel made of conchshell, oyster-shell, crystal,

bell-metal or of silver and other precious metals, but on no account with an earthen vessel. The Varaha Purana says, that "having taken an Udumvara vessel filled with water, facing the east if on the banks of a lake, a tank, a well or a river, otherwise facing the north, with three blades of kusa, a fruit, some sesamum and a flower in it one should make the Sankalpa dropping water towards the north-east.

A hymn from the Vedas should be repeated and it is generally called the Sankalpa-Sukta. But this differs in the different Vedas and the priest repeats the Sankalpa Sukta from that Veda to which the yajaman belongs. In the case of a Sudra yajamana the Sankalpa Sukta is to be recited from the Yajur-Veda. Every ceremony is completed by repeating the name of Vishnu ten times for the expiation of any defects in the sacrifice and by solemnly offering the merits arising from the ceremony to Vishnu.

(14.) THE Tantradharaka literally means one, who observes the rules of performing a sacrifice. He is an officiating priest, whose duty is to hold the book of liturgy in hand, and to direct the pujaka or the hota priest the way in which ceremonies are to be performed, or prompting the pujaka or the hota the mantras. The hota is the priest, who offers oblations to the sacred fire. In the vedas the tantradharaka does not appear, but in his place there is the Sadasya, the director of the ceremony.

(15.) THE sub-joined is the figure of a ghata :

GHATA.

From the preceding notes it will appear that a god may be worshipped in a ghata even without an idol. It is an indispensable article in religious festivals of the Hindus the mantras for establishing it as well as those for putting on the several appendages to the ghata are different in different Vedas, and those from the Veda to which the yajamana belongs are repeated in sanctifying the ghata.

(16.) The bhutapasarana is the ceremony of removing the spirits and other beings whose presence may interfere with the performance of a religious observance. The bhutas are generally disposed of by a bali of mas and curd, and they are guarded against by scattering mustard seeds. The mustard seeds so scattered with mantras are supposed to protect the sacrificial place from evil presence, and should the bhutas transgress the boundary, these mustard seeds are said to pierce them as if with a thunderbolt. The bhutas are propitiated before every sacrifice.

A bali is an offering of any thing eatable offered to the bhutas (spirits &c.) ; it is made of mas and curd. According to the Sastras every Hindu should offer every day a bali to the Visvadevas. This bali may consist of mas and curd or of sugar and flower, and it is offered with the following mantra, Om to the universal gods, Om to the Visvadevas. Om to

Yakshna do you not destroy me. Om the gods, the men, the beasts, the birds, the siddhas, the yakshas, the reptiles, the Daityas, the Pretas, the Pisachas, and the trees, and whoever desire to have food, receive this bali offered by me. Om may the ants, the worms, the insects, and whoever are hungry being imprisoned in corporeal frames, receive this food offered by me and be satisfied. Om the bhutas and all beings be satisfied with the bali by me scattered on earth for your satisfaction. Om may the crows of Indra, Varuna and Vayu, of Soma and Nirti quarters, receive this cake by me placed on earth. Om obeisance to the crows. Om to the twin dogs Syava and Savasa the offsprings of Vivasvata (Sun, the father of Pluto) accept this cake and envy not. Om to the dogs. Om to the Chandalas, to the apostates, Om to the sins and Om to the diseases. Om to Dharmaraja Chitragupta.

(17.) Durva is the grass Cynodon dactylon, Pers, a good fodder for the cattle. It grows where no other grass will grow. It is an indispensable article in Hindu ceremonies. It is said to be the hairs of Vishnu torn off by the friction of the great serpent Vasuki against his body whilst churning the ocean for nectar. It has been immortalized by nectar which when churned out from the ocean was placed by the gods on a turf of Durva. In religious ceremonies shoots of Durva with three blades on them are used. A particular day of the year is observed as sacred to Durva, and the Vrata is called Durvashtami or the eighth day of the moon sacred to Durva. In offering Durva, to the gods the central tender leaf stock is plucked out, and the head with three lower blades is selected, but in offering the same to the goddesses a head with three blades including the central one is used. It is used together with grains of paddy in blessing persons and it constitutes the principal ingredient of an arghya. It must accompany every handful of flower presented to the gods. In the Sastras it is regarded as the compendium and essence of all flowers, and the flower offering therefore is not complete without it ; in the same way the bell is considered as the compendium of all music, and in every ceremony therefore the bell is rung. Some flowers are not acceptable to certain gods, thus the mallika (Jasminum undulatum), the malati (Aganosma Roxhurghi), the yati (Jasminum grandiflorum), the kunda (Jasminum hirsutum), the sephalika (Nyctanthes arbor-tristis), the java (Hibiscus rosa-sinensis), the kamini (Muraya exotica) and the like are never to be offered to Siva : nor the java and the yantra flowers to Vishnu. The yantra flowers are the java, the aparajita (Clitoria ternata), the baka, (Agati grandiflorani), and the karavi (Nerium odoratum). The lotus and the karavi though yantra flowers may however be presented to all the gods. A yantra flower, is that whose form is like that of the *yantra*. Leaves of tulasi (Ocimum vellosum) should be offered only to Vishnu. But the leaves of amalaki (Myrobalans emblika) and vel (Ægle marmelos) may be offered to the Devi as well as to Siva. The vakula (Mimsops elengi) though a yantra flower may be offered to Vishnu.

Flowers are unfit ior presentation to the gods if they are more than 24 hours old, but the following are not considered as withered, viz. the vel leaves, Jasminum multiflorum, leaves of Phyllanthus emblica, and Xanthocymus pictorius, Nymphœa alba, tulasi, the lotus, Agati grandiflorani and sephalika ; nor are the buds of any other flowers.

---

(18) ARGHYA is derived either from Arha to worship or from Argha to cost. It constitutes a part of the worship of a god. It consists of water, durva, rice, flowers and chandana. The modes of establishing it have been described in the text. It is evidently a Tantric rite, though the practice of presentation of

something in the shape of price or puja obtained in the Pauranic Age. With arghya one is welcomed. The various mantras given in the text only mystify the performance and thus impart a solemn air to the act. The triangle is one of the yantras or mystic symbols of Sakti or Force or the female generative power, and plays an important part in the Tantric rites. As the stand for the conchshell is made three legged the triangle is the proper figure to form its base. The tripod is selected of all other forms, because it has the least number of legs with which a stand may be made steady at all places and because three is the mystic number of the Tantras. The system of worship enjoined by the Tantras being based on symbols the Sustaining Force is worshipped as the power which sustains all matter. The Adhara Sakti literally the sustaining force, has been personified in the Tantras as a female goddess. This personation of every species of force is however in the abstract philosophical, though owing to the metaphorical character of the primitive language and the prevailing ignorance of the people in the dark ages of Sanskrit literature every philosophic idea was regarded as a Divine attribute, and magnified into a god-head. The tirthas or holy places are said to reside in the solar sphere, and they are invoked by the priest raising the fore-finger in hook form. Possibly the philosophy of this ceremony is that the sun absorbs the water from all parts of the world, and that if there is any place in Heaven where the tirthas may be supposed to be found collected together, it must be in the all-absorbent sun. The Arghya is established in a conchshell, of which a figure is subjoined :

TRIPOD AND CONCHSHELL.

In the special arghya the sphere of fire is worshipped in the tripod, which is made of metal, the Solar sphere is worshipped in the conchshell and the Lunar sphere in the water.

(19.) Asana is a carpet or seat on which the worshipper sits while performing any ceremony. The Sastras say that no person while performing a ceremony should sit without an asana, an uttariya or upper vestment and a head dress. The asana is purified by the mantra given in the text. It is noteworthy that the Rshi or author of the seat-mantra is Meruprshtha literally meaning convex-backed, the upper surface of an ordinary seat of wood called Pinde in Bengali. The measure of the mantra is Sutala, literally meaning level-bottomed to secure the stable equilibrium of the seat. The lord of asana is Kurma the great tortoise said to uphold the earth on its back. The manifestation of force in a seat is the Sustaining Force, and she is therefore styled the lotus-seated as the most delicate of all seats.

(20.) This is a symbolical purification of the body. It is supposed that sin in the form of a black person is located in the left cavity of the thorax, and it is consumed together with the corporeal body of the worshipper by the fire generated by the retention or exhalation of breath for sometime. It may be observed that this ancient idea coincides with the modern theory of Correlation of the Physical Forces, the suspension of vital force generating light and heat. It may not be out of place to mention here that a similar rite is observed by the Mahomedans at the conclusion of each prayer with short addresses to the two ferishtas or good and evil spirits residing in the two sides of the body, the evil spirit residing in the left. The left side is the origin of evil according to the Hebrew scripture, and with the left rib Eve the mother of sin was created. In the cavity of the skull are supposed to be situated a thousand petalled lotus and the moon, from which distil drops of nectar, and with this nectar are rebuilt the several organs of the body; which thus formed is considered free from former vices and fit for any ceremony. It is a symbolical Tantric rite enjoined evidently for the composition of the mind before the performance of a ceremony.

The shatchakras or spheres are as follows:

1st. The muladhara (the coccyx or the anus with the several muscles of the rectum ?) an organ in the form of a quadrupetalous lotus having the formula Vasa (base or seat) consisting of four letters Va, Sa Sha, and Sa, inscribed on the four leaves representing four gods.

2nd. The Svadhishthana the organ with the uterine canal in the form of a hexapetallous lotus, having the formula Bala (force, agency) in the centre and the letters Ba, Bha, Ma, Ya, Ra, and La inscribed on its six petals.

3rd. Manipura the abdominal organ resembling a ten-petalled lotus with the formula Dapha in its pericarp and the ten letters form da to pha inscribed on its ten leaves. The region below the diaphragm is the chief characteristic of Mammalian myology, being equally developed both in Man and in the Monotreme. This is supposed in the Tantras to be like a full-blown inverted lotus, as it is vaulted and convex towards the thorax; and to have ten petals, for the diaphragm consists of carneous and tendinous parts, the latter chiefly in the expanded and aponeurotic form, the carneous fasciculi being divided into "costal" or greater and the 'vertebral' or smaller muscles, the costal portions arising from the ensiform cartilege and those of the eighth to the twelvth ribs connected by fasciculi, which interdigitate with those of the 'transversalis abdominis' muscle. The orifice through which jivatma (corporeal soul) passes upwards towards the Paramatma (the Divine spirit) is situated between the right and the middle tracts, for the inferior vena cava (' post caval' of Mammals) passes through it. Behind the tendon and to the left of the median line (for the aponeurocis called ' centrum tendineum' or ' cordiform tendon' is widely notched towards the spine and divided anteriorly into three tracts, of which the right is usually the largest) is also located another orifice for the œsophagus and pneumogastric nerves. The aorta also passes from the chest to the abdomen between the ' crura' of the lesser muscle. It is difficult however now to guess which of these passages are referred to by the Tantras. Is it one for the ' Vena cava ?'

4th. Anahata the chest-like, a duodecafolea lotus, having the formula Katha with its twelve letters from ka to tha marked on each leaf.

5th. Visuddha the vocal organ in the throat likened to a sixteen-petalled lotus, the sixteen vowels with the nasal anusvaras inscribed on each petal.

6th. Ajna a bipetalous lotiform organ between the eye-brows with the letters Ha and Ksha inscribed on two petals.

7th- The Brahma randhra or the divine orifice the anterior superior fontanelle. The unclosed suture of the frontal bones in the new-born child is covered with the skin, which is heaved up and depressed at each vibration of the heart. This is filled up by the formation of Warmian-bones and the marks of these sutures are left in the skull even after death. These marks are likened by the Tantras to a mille-petalled lotus retentive of the marks of a thousand characters.

8th. Kailasa the cranium or seat of Mahadeva.

(21.) Nyasa literally means setting or placing of articles in their proper localities. According to the

Tantras the several letters of the alphabet are supposed to represent the several Matrika divinities (see Note 47.) or sustainers of our corporeal organs, the functions of the same being considered as so many forces or saktis of the Matrikas. The Matrikas therefore are the deifications of the several Physiological Forces viewed in the light of the Tantras The letters of the alphabet being the ultimate particles with which thoughts are expressed, are considered to possess attributes supernatural and unknowable. The Word of god, the Vedas, is considered as eternal, indeed co-existent with the Deity, whence the Mimansa aphorism "Savdo yonitvat Brahman" sound is increate Brahman. It is not therefore unnatural to suppose that the authors of the Tantras, who viewed every thing with an eye of mysticism should have indulged in high mystics and transcendental speculations peculiar to the dark ages of the world.

The proper location of the several letters of the alphabet as symbols of the saktis (forces) in the several parts of the body over which the Matrika Saktis (Physiological Forces) are supposed to preside is the Matrika Nyasa.

(22.) ড ফ, ক ঠ, Dapha, Katha are not as may be supposed single vijas or roots consisting ot the letters da, pha, ka, and tha, but are formula expressing a concatenation or series of vijas or roots. They are mantras or mnemoniac syllables of certain female deities indicated by the two (initial and final) letters togethei with those coming between them. In the same way the Samketika Samahara of Vopadeva or indicatory figures or modes of logicians or abbreviated Pratyahara terminology of Panini stands for the letters indicated by them. Accordingly Dapha expresses ten letters of the alphabet commencing from da and ending with pha. Dapha meaning the ocean fire (latent heat) being fanned by the storm wind, a symbolical expression of the vital heat being generated by respiration. This formula is the compendium of all the symbols connected with vitality or life or existence of a being and its seat is therefore the navel, the terminus of the cord, which nourished the fœtal being when in the womb of the mother (Matrika). But the pha of Dapha is permutable in grammar to pa and bha, its homogeneous soft and hard sounds which make Dapa, and Dabha both meaning a heap or collection (of food) deposited in the stomach and concocted into chyle by the [presiding deities represented by da (Siva as latent heat), pha (Sivani as digestive wind) and others. Katha similarly stands for the twelve consonants from ka to tha. Katha means sound made by the movement of the respiratory organs *i. e.* Hansa and Soham. These two formula are Sacred to two Antarmatris, inherent in two of the six spheres or zones or regions of the human body, and the letters implied by them appertain to the minor saktis or forces residing in those two parts of the human frame, which is on that account emphatically styled the microcosm or mundane monad or rather the *corpus deorum* of the Pythagoreans.

These two parts are the Manipura or the abdominal circle, navel or the seat of fœtal life, and the anahata, or the region of the heart, the seat of the extra-uterine life. The Matris Vaishnavi the goddess of cupidity and Rudrani of fury residing in these regions are called Mahamatrikas, by reason of their important functions both in the fœtal and subsequent conditions, that is of assimilating food into blood in the latter, and vivifying the corporeal frame by the distribution of the vital fluid in the former.

It may be observed that the Anandalahari of Sankaracharya in praise of 'Siva, conjoined with Sakti,' his Energy, in her different forms of the Matris in the six spheres of the human-body, is the most elegant metaphysical poem that has ever been written on the subject. Its commentator Jagadisa has explained how from each couplet the Vija for each form of Sakti commencing with Hansa, the Vija for Tripurasundari, could be derived. Ramaprasada, the great Sakta poet, has composed many songs on the meditation of the Six spheres and contemplation of the universe within one's self. He commences one of them as follows:

কুল কুণ্ডলিনী ব্রহ্মময়ী আছে গো অদূরে।

মূলাধার স্বাধিষ্ঠান, মণিপূর নাভি স্থান, বিশুদ্ধা-

জ্ঞবরে।।

---

(23) Phat is the vija or root of destructive weapons, agreeing with the Arabic Fat (death, destruction.) It is pronounced in washing and purifying the Santipot, the arghya vessel, and the sacrificial vases; in invoking the removal of all hinderances, heretics and unbelievers, and in several other ceremonies. It is also used as a mantra in Tantric rites for the removal of evil spirits &c. Similarly the mantras Sphyem, Sphoum and such other derivatives of the noun Sphyam literally meaning a wooden sword, perhaps the primitive sword of the aborigines, and mostly used in despatching sacrificial animals according to the Tantras.

Svaha is a mantra uttered before offering an oblation of ghi to the fire. It is described in the 37th chapter of the Bhrama Vaivartha Purana as the daughter of Brahma and as the wife of Agni. The story of her origin is as follows. The gods after creation having nothing to eat became hungry and applied to Brahma for food. Brahma thereupon meditated on Vishnu, who forthwith assumed the form of Sacrifice, Yajna under the name of Yajnesvara presiding over all sacrifices, and consumed all ghi offered to fire, instead of sharing it with the gods. The latter again applied to Brahma complaining of Vishnu's behaviour, whereupon Brahma once more meditated on (Force) the female attribute of Vishnu, and she appeared to Brahma as Svaha, and at Brahma's request married Agni, and as his attribute, consuming flame, she bore away all oblations made to fire for the gods.

Svadha is the daughter of Daksha or according to some of Brahma. She is married to the Pitrs, and bears away all oblations offered to the pitrs or the departed.

Vashat, Vaushat, and such other mantras are used in offering oblations of ghi to fire. They are much used in the Tantras in the several Nyasas.

In the Taittiriya Aranyaka of the Black Yajurveda, fourth Book, several mantras are given as meet for the Pravargya Homa, the fire for which is lighted with thorny faggots and in section 28 of the same the following imprecatory phrases occur, *viz.*, Khat, Phat, Jahi, Chhindhi, Bhindhi, Handhi, Kat &c., and these are said in the text to be maledictory. The derivation of these phrases may be traced to the roots implying to split, to remove, to sever to pierce, to destroy, and to cut. Sayanacharya the Commentator says that these sounds imply threat. Khat and the two following are words imitative of the sounds used in threatening. And the rest are verbs for killing in the imperative mood. These six are harsh sounds.

The Taittiriya Brahman in Book 2, Chapter 1, Section 2 gives an anecdote of the origin of Svaha. It runs thus. In the beginning Prajapati the Creator created Agni, who having nothing to eat applied to Him but in vain, and consequently attacked Creator with his fellow creatures. Prajapati, however, to avoid Agni retreated backwards but failed to stop him, and in the exertion thus made felt fatigued and wiped off the sweat of his brow His sweat became ghi and being not certain as to its purity (being an execration) for offering the same to Agni as an oblation held the same in his right hand and mentally asked the question what it is, and a voice from heaven announced Svaham (Sva-Aham) I am thyself, and whereupon Prajapati repeating the word Svaham offered the oblation to Agni. Hence Svaha is the root of Homa, and is pronounced as a mantra in offering oblations to fire. Vashat is used in the Taittirya Brahman in the same sense as Khat, Phat &c., in the Taittirya Aranyaka. TheCommentator adds Vashat is to be uttered after the ten imprecatory phrases mentioned above at the end of a sacrifice for the final destruction of enemy.

The Taittiriya Brahman relates an interesting anecdote regarding the origin of the word Vashat. The God presiding over Vashat is Vashatkara. The anecdote is as follows. Once upon a time Vrhaspati struck the goddess Gayatri on the head, which was smashed into pieces and the brain spilt. But Gayatri is immortal, and every drop of her brain so spilt was alive and became Vashatkara. The Commentator adds Vashat is derived from Vasa, grease, brain-matter. The sa of Vasa preceding the celebral ta is changed into sha. It may be mentioned that Vrhaspati is the planet Jupiter and also the teacher of the gods. He is also the author of the Charvak (atheistic) philosophy, which it is said was invented by him to mislead the Asuras, the enemies of the gods. Vrhaspati is the wisest among both the immortals and mortals. The Gayatri, the sacred formula of the Hindus, the mantra which is repeated in the daily service, has been personified into a Goddess of the same name, who is invoked and worshipped morning and evening.

The anecdote stripped of its metaphorical garb implies as follows. The atheists, ignorant of the meaning of the mantra and not recognising the excellent principle inculcated by the words contained in it, regarded it as a mere collection of certain labial sounds, which in contempt they typified by va, sa, and ta. Indeed the Gayatri consists of 9 labial consonants, 9 dentals, 3 dental ses, and 8 other consonants, five of which again have the labial vowels attached to them.

Vrhaspati therefore was not far from the point when he called Gayatri as a concatenation of the letters va, sa, and ta in the same way that some critic patting Vyasa, the author of the Mahabharata, on the belly said it was filled with cha, vai, tu, and hi, meaningless monads profusely introduced by Vyasa in his great epic to preserve the measures of his lines. The dental sounds are considered soft sounds, and as such they are rarely used to express angry sentiments or harsh words. The cerebral equivalents are used to express imprecations. Hence vasata has been changed into Vashat. To call such a sacred mantra as the Gayatri by so low a name as Vashat is to strike on the head of Gayatri and the constituent brain-matter thus spilt represents the syllables. From the above it will be seen that these words are sounds imitative of the cruel actions indicated by them, and are therefore used in invoking the removal of evil spirits or sin from one's own person or in despatching sacrifices.

(24.) Pitha literally means the seat (see Note 50.) The Pitha Nyasa is therefore the location of several Energies or deities presiding over the several parts of the body. In performing the Pitha Nyasa the several great seats or props of the earth according to the Hindu cosmogony are invoked. Prakrti is Nature, Kurma is supposed to hold Vasuki (Ananta) the great serpent on its back, and Ananta to hold the earth on its hoods. The tortoise is said to swim on the ocean, but the ocean of milk here referred to as being seated in the thorax is evidently an allegorical expression for chyme which is the first step gained by Vital Force towards the assimilation of food and the conversion of vegetable into animal organism. The sternum in a human skeleton located as it is above the region of the stomach must have suggested the idea of a white island.

The Kalpa tree is one of the "propria" of the deity. The tree is said to give any thing that is asked of it. In primitive ages when the fruit yielding tree and the milk-yielding cow constituted the only properties man had, the Kalpa tree and the Kama Dhenu were regarded as the proper possessions of the deity.

"Whatever goeth in doth not defile a man but whatever cometh out of the mouth defileth him." The mouth is therefore the source of unrighteousness.

Right (rectus) represents the rightness of a thing and left (sinister) the wrongness, and the seat of Dharma (Virtue) is therefore the right side and that of Sin the left. But why is the left shoulder regarded as the seat of intelligence? It is observable that the sacerdotal thread which distinguishes, the Brahman from the Sudra, the knowing caste from the unknowing, is placed on the left shoulder.

The navel is the part of the body, through which the vital fluid is circulated for the sustenance of the fœtus, and it is therefore held to be the passage, through which 'worldliness' enters the body of the fœtus.

The sun is said to have twelve phases for it passes through the twelve signs of the zodiac to complete the cycle of the year. Similarly the moon has sixteen phases or digits. The sacrificial fire in the Dasahotra Yajna is said to be of ten kinds. The several phases of Agni are named in the Taittiriya Aranyaka under Chaturhotra and other sacrifices.

(25.) The upacharas are articles of worship, they are sixty in number viz., the carpet, perfumed oil, the bath, the seat in the bath room, pure water, ointment, warm water, water of holy places in a gold vessel, a white napkin, red wearing vestment, red wrapper, painted hall, painted seat, pomades, unguent ointment of sandal, agallocha, croccus, camphor, musk, rochana (a substitute of turmeric, it is the bilious secretion of the bull), garlands made of blossoms of several season flowers such as the several jasmines, champaca &c., ornaments, jewelled seat, gemmed crown, canopy, vermilion, tilaka, collyrium, earrings, nose-rings, rouge for the lips (misi), necklace, gold sabbots, silver sandals, pearl-necklaces, a single necklace, breast plate, four bracelets, wrist-rings, finger-rings, gold-zones, girdle, sobha, anklets, nupuras, toe-rings, noose, goad, bow, arrow, crystal foot-stool, lion-seat, bed-stead, spoon, water for washing the face, camphor pills, joyous smiles, lustrations, white umbrella, chauris, mirror, fan, perfumes, flowers, incenses, lamps, eatables, water for washing and for ablution, betel leaves, and prayer.

These are abridged into thirty-six, eighteen, sixteen, ten, and sometimes five article according to the varying circumstances of worshippers. The Bhavishya Purana says that puja made without a sacrifice leads to famine, without sandal unguent to misfortune, without incense to anxiety, and without apparel to poverty. TheKurma Purana adds the following offerings. viz., cocoa-nuts, betel-nuts, pomegranates, syrup of emblica, frumenty, cakes, barley bread, wheat bread, sweetmeats, and several confections of ghi and rice, boiled with ghi and sugar, all kinds of curries, milk, curd, whay, fresh cheese, and butter, of cow and buffalo milk. Rice and curry cooked by Brahmans even in the house of a Sudra might be offered to Durga together with, says the Satatapa Brahman, meats of different kinds.

Each article of offering is lorded by a god, and in presenting the same to any god or goddess the lord of the article should be worshipped, together with the article and the god or goddess to whom the same is offered. This ceremony is called the archana of the article. The Sastras say that the offering of an article accompanied by an archana is meritorious both to the donor and the donee.

The gods who preside over the several articles are as follows: Moon is the lord of silver, Vrhaspati of cloth, Varuna of water, Vanaspati of flower, Gandharva of incense, Agni of goat, Varuna of sheep, Yama or Bhairava of buffalo, Kurma of carpet, Agni of gold, &c. &c. and Vishnu of all. Indeed in ordinary ceremonies the Brahmans generally name Vishnu as the lord of the articles offered. But the Vedas give a different list of the lords of articles. In the Taittiriya Brahman B II. the following anecdote regarding the orgin of the lords of articles and the necessity of their mediation in the presentation of articles to gods is given. The gods themselves had at one time officiated as priests at a sacrifice made by Varuna and received several sacrificial articles as their fees or honorarium for the service rendered. The acceptance of these direct gifts (*i. e.* without intervention of a third person) made the gods sick, whereupon they caused a mutual transfer of the gifts, which changing hands brought back their health. It may be here noted that a gift is not quite so meritorious to the donee as it is to the donor.

Hence the naming the lord of an article before it is given away protects the receiver from the injurious effects of receiving a direct gift. The acceptance of a gift by a god or a priest is held to be an acceptance of the thing by the divinity. Thus gold was given to Agni who gave it back to another god and hence Agni is called the lord of gold. Similarly cloth to the Moon, cow to Rudra, water to Varuna, person to Prajapati, bed to Manu, bedstead to Angirasa. The commentator adds that gold was given to Agni on account of the resemblance of his color to the brilliancy of the metal, and white vestment to Soma, the moon, for the same reason.

The Tantras view things in an allegorical and philosophical light. The manasa puja or worship with mental offerings substituted for the tangible rice, the tangible flower &c., is a necessary adjunct to the bhutasuddhi, &c. processes meant but for composing of the mind. The Tantras however are not singular in prescribing mental worship. The Vedas also in the Taittirya Aranyaka have identified mind, speech &c. with the several articles of sacrifice.

The Ramayana mentions that Ramachandra having vowed to worship Durga with one lac of lotus flowers and finding one of them missing plucked out one of his eye-balls and offered it as a substitute. Such transcendental devotion and piety sometimes overpower common sense and lead the jealous devotee to offer even the blood of his body as an acceptible offering to the deity.

(26.) THE Muses or six sentiments of Hindu composition are the Sringara (erotic), the Hasya (ludicrous), the Karuna (pathetic) the Vira (heroic), the Rudra (vehement) and the Bhayanaka (terrific). Some add the Adbhuta (marvellous) and the Vibhatsa (Batyric).

---

(27) THE Devi Mahatmya is a portion of the Markandeya Purana. In it are described several incarnations of the Devi, and the battles she fought, the demons she destroyed as well as the forms in which she was worshipped, and the meritorious effects which follow worship. It is ordinarily called the Chandi. It is recited with certain other mantras called the argala, the kilaka, the kavacha &c.

The Chandipatha or the reading of the Devi Mahatmya from the Markandeya Purana is performed by first reading the Argala (the bolt), the Kilaka (the spine) and the Kavacha (the armour) of the Devi

Mahatmya. Some peculiarities should be observed in reading the Chandi. The reading should not be too loud nor so low as not to be audible from a hundred yards. It should not be read fast nor so slow as to impair the sense of what is read. The book in the pothi form should be placed upon a raised table and the cloth round the waist should be slightly loosened.

The rshi of the first part is Brahma, the Goddess, is Mahakali, the metre is Gayatri, the Sakti is Narada the root Raktadantika, and the meaning Agni. Mahakali is described as ten-faced, ten-armed, and black as the beetle or lamp-black, she is decorated with thirty large eyes, her teeth protrude beyond her lips, she is terrific and fierce, she holds a sword, a dart, a mace, an arrow, an iron crow-bar ; a club, a javelin, a bow, a skull, and a goad, she was born in the war of Madhukaitabha and was turn black.

Vishnus is the rshi of the middle portion, of Devi Mahatmya, the goddess is Mahalakshmi, the metre is Anustupa, the Sakti is Sakambhari, the root is Durga, and the object Surva. Mahalakshmi is described as white-faced, blue-armed, pure white-bosomed, red waisted, red-bodied, thick-thighed, full-breasted, and round-cheeked, wonderfully decorated, and possessed of all kinds of felicity, eighteen-armed ; she was worshipped in the battle of the thousand-armed.

Rudra is the rshi of the last portion, of Devi Mahatmya, Sarasvati is the goddess, Ushnika the metre, Bhima the Sakti, Bhramari the root, Vayu is the object. Sarasvati is described as born of the body of Gauri, the fountain of all merits, and the destroyer of Sumbha demon. Eight-armed and holding an arrow, a club, a dart, a discus, a conchshell, a bell, a plough, and a bow in each arm respectively. She was worshipped at the time of Sumbha and Nisumbha's destruction.

The Sastras enumerate the merits of reciting the Devi Mahatmya many times over in the following manner:

For the overcoming of hinderances men should thrice read the Chandi, for propitiating the evil influences of planets five times, for obtaining safety from imminent danger seven times, for attaining the merits of a Vajapeya sacrifice nine times and so on—

(28.)—The Arati, properly Aratrikam. It means the lustration of arms or lights presented on occasions of religious ceremonies as well as of martial rites. It is performed with lighted lamps, with lighted camphor, with white clothes, with flowers, with several sacred leaves, with a mirror, with a chauri, and with several other things. The great Nirajana, which is celebrated in North Western Province on the occasion of Dasahara is performed on the 19th day of Asvina. The Sastras enjoin. Then with the mulamantra offer three handsful of flowers, make the great nirajana with joyous sound and music, and light ghi or camphor in good Aratrikm (lamps for lustration) with many tapers but uneven in number.

The Aratrika or the Arati lamp as it is called is ordinarily made of brass. It consists of a brass figure of an angel holding on her two hands a series of five chirags. The body of the angel forms the handle with which the priest holds the article. In making the arati the hall in which the idols are located is perfumed with exquisite aromatic fragrance of incenses of dhuna (resin of Shorea robusta) guggul and dhupa. The Dhupa is a composition incense, it consists of guggul, the resin of Balsamodendron agallocha, of saral, the resin of Pinus longifolia, wormwood, sandal, myrobalans, shell-lac, Nardostachys, jatamansi, and such other aromatic drugs. These are pounded together and a paste is made with ghi and molasses.

The priest having made the achaman purifies the lighted Arati lamps and takes the figure up in his right hand and gracefully moves it round before the idol, while with his left he rings a bell. The Sastras say that the lustration should not consist of less than four revolutions before the feet, not less than two before the face and not less than seven before all parts of the body, and when it is finished a lamp of lighted camphor is taken and the same number of curves is described, then the same with a piece of white cloth, a flower, a mirror, a chauri &c. All this while the priest rings the bell, and other parties sound the gong, a conchshell and several other instruments.

In the Durgotsava the Aratrika is generally a well shaped small candelabra of silver, bearing several lamps :

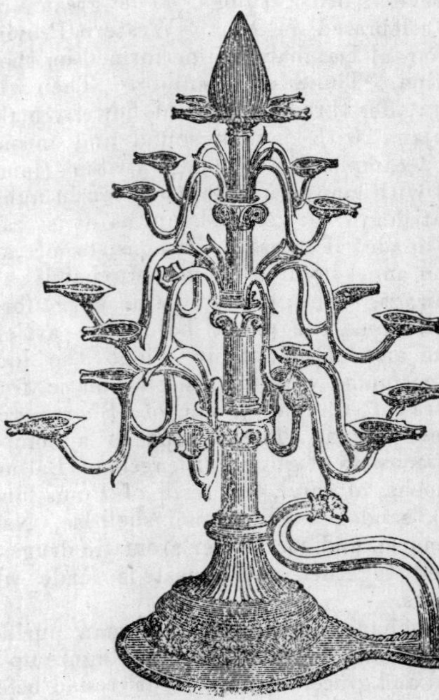

ARATRIKA.

The arati is celebrated with great eclat, all the members of the family being assembled stand in regular lines by the piers leaving the opening between the arches free to the view of the crowd which collect in the courtyard, the worship hall where the Devi is seated, and in the aisles. Several Brahmans are engaged to swing the chauris before the goddess, and these generally stand on both sides of the goddess. The devotees clapped their hands in musical cadence and recite in devotional tunes prayers in Sanskrit, drums, dhols, and dhaks beat in the courtyard while the Nahovat and the Roshana-chaukis play at their respective places. Three priests perform the Arati with three sets of Aratrikas and three bells. After the arati is over a circumambulation is made and the priests then prostrate themselves before the goddess.

At the time of Arati certain musical instruments are prohibited to be used in the worship of certain gods. The Yogini Tantra says, that in the house of Siva cymbals should not be rung, nor should the conchshell be blown in the hall of Surya, nor the bamboo flute in that of Durga. The Matsya Purana adds, avoid the drum in the temple of Brahma, and the bell in that of Lakshmi. The arati should be always accompanied with songs and the music of instruments, but where the poor worshipper cannot afford for expensive music, he can substitute the bell which is considered the compendium of all music.

The great arati festival of the Devi is performed on the morning of the Dasami when the Devi is prayed to retire. The Puja Ratnakara says that the goddess is to be respectfully lustrated with figures made of pounded rice, with lamps, with the twigs of the religious fig tree and other trees, with medicinal drugs and balsams &c., accompanied by the blowing of conchshells, the beating of drums, and shouts of victory.

(29.) ADHIVASA literally means the fumigation of a person or god with incenses. It is a peculiar rite observed on the evening preceding certain ceremonies. Thus the bridegroom is said to have his adhivasa before his marriage. It is something like the preparation of the person to be worshipped or blessed. It is a preliminary to the auspicious ceremonies as Sanjama is to Sraddha. The articles with which adhivasa of Durga is performed are enumerated in Note (44.)

(30.) SVASTICA literally means auspicious. Svastica is made of dough of rice. It is moulded by Brahman ladies and painted yellow. It is supposed to represent the generative principle of the deity. It is shaped like a triangle. It forms a part of the Sri, a figure of which is subjoined :

SRI.

Sri is supposed to represent the mount Meru. It is an auspicious article. It is painted yellow, red and purple at parts.

(31.) THE details given in the performance of the preliminary pujas are daily repeated in practice. Every day the usual achamana, the bhuta and asana suddhis, the nyasas, the pranayama and the worship of the sun and five other gods are observed. On the saptami day the idols are vivified, their life is supposed to continue till the gods represented by the idols are requested to retire. One goat sacrifice is generally offered on the Saptami day.

---

(32).—THE Snana is the solemn anointing of a deity with drugs, cosmetics, and waters from various tirthas or holy places. The Snana of the Navapatricas (a figure of which is given on the cover) is observed with some solemnity, for the Sastras say, he who anoints the Goddess with great eclat and pomp attains beatitude. The first article used in the bathing of the Goddess is an ointment of turmeric and oil. The people of certain parts of Bengal, specially, those of the eastern districts up to this day anoint their body with turmeric and oil before they go to bathe. The turmeric is considered useful in many respects, firstly because it is supposed to be a preventive of attacks of crocodiles, which abound in most of the rivers of Bengal; secondly because it is a vermifuge; thirdly because it paints the body yellow and according to taste tickles the fancy.

The several attributes named in the text are invoked to anoint the Goddess. This is done metapohrically. The Goddess as it were is blessed with the attributes.

Similarly in anointing, her with infusion of flowers she is said to be anointed with the drugs of the Asvini Kumaras, the physicians of the Gods, with the essential glory of Brahma the Deity, with drugs of Sarasvati and with the organ of organs (mind).

Sarasvati is here meant for the Goddess of the river of the same name. In the Rig Veda however Sarasvati is described as a great sea, full of all sacrifices, beautified with variously formed fishes, and presides over the seas, she is the repository of all drugs and jewels, for in the Sastras the sea is said to be jewel-wombed.

Cocoanut water is offered with the mantra Hrim Phat to the weapons, a very proper mantra for cutting the fruit with a catan.

The sahasradhara is an earthen bowl used in bathing gods. It has at its bottom many small holes through which water falls in thousand currents like those from the rose of a shower-bath.

Bathing with eight jars of water. The first filled with Ganga water is said to be poured by the gods, as the Ganga is supposed to be a continuation of the Heavenly stream, the Mandakini. The rain water is supposed to be poured by the gods of clouds, as they raise water to the clouds which pour the same on the earth by condensing it. The Vidyadharas are supposed to pour Sarasvati water, as Sarasvati is also the goddess of the Muses. Indra, the lord of the firmament and the gods presiding over the ten quarters are said to pour sea water as they are the likely lords of the high sea.

The five tonics are barks of Mimusops elengi, Acacia arabica, Syzigium Jambolana, Zizyphus jujuba, and Sida cordifolia. These are all medicinal plants, and the decoction of these is used as astringent and mucilagenous drinks in dysentery and like diseases.

Kakkol commonly called Kankla or Kankhra in Bengal is a small roundish aromatic fruit of Hydralea Zeylanica.

(33.) **Mana** is a noble arum much used by the natives in their curries. It is worshipped in certain parts of Bengal under the name of Managiri or Managosvami, for further particulars connected with tree-worship see J. A. S. B. Vol. XXXIX. part P. p 212 et seq.

(34.) THE Hindu Sastras enumerate seven great oceans encircling the seven great continents into which they divide the earth. The oceans are described in the Vedas as being raised by the moon, indeed one of the names of ocean in Sanskrit (Samudra) is derived from Chandra at whose rise it (ocean) heaves up. Some however have translated the Sanskrit word Samudra into sea, perhaps laying a great stress on the last portion of the word Sa-Mudra, thoroughly encompassed by land.

The gods and the demons are said to have churned nectar out of the ocean. In the great anointing of the Navapatrica, sea water is used because the sea is the receiver of the water of holy rivers and therefore regarded as a compendium of all tirthas.

(35.) ACCORDING to the Sastras the river Ganga is said to be present in the heavens, in the earth, as well as in the nether worlds. In the heavens it is known by the name of Mandakini, which is said to have sprung from the feet of Vishnu and hence called the Vishnu torrent. Its glory is great, because it is the only stream in all India, which supplies a pure and wholesome beverage from its source to its fall. This river is said to have been brought down to the earth by Bhagiratha a prince of the solar race of Kshatriyas and the Ganga in the earth therefore is called the Bhagirathi. The Ganga in the nether worlds is called Bhogavati from which water was raised for Bhisna Deva, the Nestor of the Kauravas, in his last moments, by Arjuna, who pierced the lower region with an arrow.

L

The milky way in the heavens seemed to have suggested the idea of the existence of a river in the upper regions, and the inaccessible sources of the Ganges lost in the higher peaks of the Himavat favored this idea. The heavenly torrent is said to have gushed forth from the feet of the god of day, whose one name is Vishnu, because the milky way follows the track of the sun.

The Pauranic idea of the Ganga is that it is the liquification of a mass of matter by the glory of Vishnu (the sun.) Does it refer to the melting of the ice on the Hemavat by the rays of the sun or does it mean the liquification of that which is absorbed by the sun, or to express in the language of science the liquified sun, for such indeed is the Sanskrit phrase? Possibly our ancestors traced the ubiquitous Ganga in the nether worlds to the springs, which came from below.

(36.) WARM water is considered medicinal in bathing, but for drinking the Sastras enjoin water that is pure, free from bubbles, cold and transparent. The water for bathing Durga should not be too hot nor too cold. The Sastras say, water should be such as not to produce the sensation of cold or heat when touched or in other words it should be equal to the temperature of the body. The mantras to be repeated in using hot water are numerous. The Taittiriya Aranyaka under head of Pravargya mantras has the following mantra, which is recited when warm water is poured over the body of the yajamana :

Om may the wind residing in space bless us, may the sun bless us with his cheering rays, Om may the days be pleasant to us. May Usha Devi bid us a good morning, may Aditya (the sun) rise for our prosperity &c. &c. &c.

(37.) In earlier days there were two modes of extracting the perfumes of flowers. The one was by the infusion of flowers in water, and the other by boiling the same in water. The former being the easier and cheaper of the two was frequently resorted to. But in the advanced days of Kalidasa the extract of flowers was much in vogue. Kalidasa pronounces benediction to his readers at the end of the first canto of his poem on the seasons saying, may you pass the evening hours of the hot season sprinkling your person with the fragrant infusion of lotuses and the essence of roses &c. &c.

The Asvina Kumaras are the twin physicians of the gods, and they are therefore invoked to anoint the Devi with drugs and infusions of flowers. Sarasvati is the goddess of a river of that name as well as of the ocean, and she is therefore invoked to anoint the Devi with her marine drugs.

(38.) The five Gabyas or bovine articles so much prized in Hindu religious ceremonies are the cow dung, the cow-urine, the milk, the curd, and the clarified butter from cow-milk. They are used in anointing a Salagram, in purifying a polluted Vigraha or idol, and in expiating certain pollutions.

Cow-dung is considered a great purifier, and the kitchen and the place where the dinner is taken are daily washed with cow-dung. Bull-dung however is quite useless for such purposes. Cow-urine is also a purifier but not quite so, though it is valued for its medicinal properties. It contains a good proportion of ammonia and one or two tea spoonsful are often administered in cases of new fevers.

(39.) Tank water of the text is evidently the water of what is called Bandhs in the West Burdwan Districts. Tanks in Lower Bengal are excavated, while the Bandhs or tanks, of the Sastras, "in which water from hills are retained permanently," are reservoirs of water formed on the slopes of hills by the erection of mounds or embankments on the sloping sides. The water during the rains and even afterwards coming down the hills is retained within the enclosure.

(40.) THE goddess is anointed with ten kinds of earth. This is evidently a symbolical anointing of the goddess with meritorious or virtuous actions which are said to reside in the earth.

The earth from the banks of a river is supposed to contain the meritorious actions of persons who cross it, similarly the earth from the doors of a prostitute, for in the Sastras it is said that the virtues of a person entering a prostitute's house are deposited on the threshold.

The Taittiriya Aranyaka enjoins the use of earth dug up by the tusk of a boar and piled by the ants in the construction of the Mahavira pot for the sacrifice and the commentator adds that the use of the earth dug by the tusk of a boar is typical of the sacrifices bearing away the ill-luck of the Yajamana in the same manner the Boar incarnation of Vishnu held the earth on its tusk. The earth from ant hills similarly typifies the strength of such minute insects.

(41.) THE Rgas are the modes of the Hindus for a complete analysis of the same see Sir W. Jones' Works Vol. I. p. 428.

(42.) LAJACA is what we call Khai in Bengali. It is snow-white baked paddy. It is considered as a light food for the sick, and being very light in weight is easily scattered and blown about by the slightest puff of wind. It is scattered on occasions of festivity and merry making.

It is an ancient preparation of rice and is mentioned in the Vedas as a necessary article in the Homa for Asvamedha Sacrifice. The ten articles prescribed for the Asvamedha are ghi or clarified butter, honey, rice, flattened rice (chipitaka, chire), baked rice (khai), powdered barley mixed with clarified butter, fried barley-meal, baked barley, masusi and grains of Panicum italicum.

(43.) On the fourth (Chaturthi) day the madhuparka, the tilaka, and the collyrium are dedicated to the goddess. The madhuparka literally means a confection of honey. It is a food of the gods. It consists of honey, ghi, curd and sugar. No worship is complete without it, and all the gods are equally pleased with it. It is an ancient confection and is said to have been invented by Brahma. It is presented to the gods in a cup, and in the Durgotsava the principal idols viz. Ganesa, Kartikeya, Siva, Narayana, Ramachandra, the Asura, the lion, the serpent, the peacock, the mouse, and Sarasvati and Lakshmi are daily worshipped with this confection in new brazen cups, which are appropriated by the officiating priests. The Devi however is presented with this delicious confection in a silver cup and the principal officiating priest takes it. It is one of the sixteen articles of offering. Many are of opinion that it is a Tantric composition, but it can be traced to the age of the Aranyaka and the Brahmans of the Vedas, for in Taittiriya Aranyaka of the Black Yajur Veda, the mantras for preparing the same and offering it to Agni are given. Sayanacharya says, honey is mixed with curd in the cup and the following mantra is pronounced : "O Dharma, this curd mixed with honey

&c. is thy food, this cup also is full with curd mixed with honey. Be thou pleased with this and being pleased bestow on us prosperity and affluence. O Dharma this full cup is thy food. It has been filled with curd mixed with honey. Curd is the best of all edibles in taste and flavour. With this tastefui, the first of foods, bless us with plenty and success."

(44.) THE Sastras say that to see the idol is meritorious but to bow to it is more meritorious than to see it and to touch it more than to bow to it, and to worship it more than to touch it. But to bathe it is more than to touch it and to offer oblations to it more than to bathe it, but the most meritorious of all is to offer the meat of buffalo and kid as sacrifice. The Bhavishya Purana says, the goddess is gratified for ten years if the blood of a goat is once offered, but that of buffalo pleases her for a hundred years. The Kalika Purana says, the goddess is propitiated for twelve years by the blood of an antelope or of a boar. But the Devi Purana says, with the blood of an antelope and of a rhinoceros Chandica is gratified for 500 years, and with the meat of Rohita fish (Cyprinus rohita) she is gratified for 300 years. The animals fit for sacrifice are the goat, the sheep, the buffalo, the rhinoceros, several kinds of deer, the tiger, and several kinds of fishes as well as the gourd and the sugar-cane, which are considered as equivalent to animal sacrifice. The animals ordinarily sacrificed, however, are the goat, the sheep and the buffalo. Some however sacrifice the fishes. The goat for sacrifice should be well formed and horned and of uniform black color.

On the day of Saptami one goat is generally sacrificed. Some do not at all offer any sacrifice on the Ashtami day. But most families sacrifice a goat on the occasion of the Sandhya Puja. The Navami is the day for abundant sacrifices. The Brahma Vaivarta Purana says, the goddess is gratified for twelve months with the blood of the iguana, she is gratified for twelve years with the blood of the antelope and the boar, and for twenty-five years with the blood of goats but for a century with the blood of buffalo and rhinoceros and she is gratified for ever with the blood of a tiger.

The Tantras quoting the Atharva Veda say that the sacrificial animal should be young, free from diseases, bearing horns, and other auspicious marks on the body, pure, well-formed and fully developed. Chandica destroys the children of those who offer too young sacrifices, the patrons of those who offer too old sacrifices, the friends of those who offer lean sacrifices, the relatives of whose who offer gigantic sacrifices, the tenants of those who offer mutilated sacrifices, the wives of those who offer sacrifices with broken horns, and the brothers of those who offer blind animals, and the sacrificer himself if the head of the sacrifice be party-colored, and again the friends of the sacrificer if the back be copper-colored and the prosperity of him who offers a tail less animal.

In the earlier days the sacrificial animals were selected with much care. Certain kinds of animals were considered fit for sacrifice to certain gods. Thus the Taittiriya Brahmana of the Black Yajur Veda enjoins the sacrifice of a white goat to Vayu the god of the winds, a castrated goat to Prajapati, a black goat with a white foot to Varuna, the grease of a sheep to Aditya, a black-necked sheep to Agni, a pregnant sheep to Indra, a dwarf cow to Vishnu, a drooping horned and thick-legged cow to Indra and Mitra.

Both the Puranas and the Tantras prohibit the sacrifice of female animal.

The animal should be despatched with one blow of a sharp sword struck on the neck. All sacrifices of animals offered by Hindus are made with a sword striking on the back of the neck and severing the head by one stroke, except those offered to Annapurna, which are slain with a knife applied to the throat. If by any mischance the head of the animal be not severed from the body by one stroke the sacrifice is considered impure and rejected. Another animal is then sacrificed and an expiatory homa is made with the flesh of the first rejected animal. Such an accident however is considered inauspicious, though in the sacrifice of a buffalo no great care is taken for that animal may be despatched with more than one blow. The Sastras permit two kinds of sacrifice, the one consisting of an animal actually slain and the other of an animal simply consecrated to the god and then let loose. The animal is slain only when the Sastras require that blood and flesh of the animal should be offered, otherwise the sword is just placed on the neck of the animal, which is considered as slain by the mere touch of it. Thus when an animal is offered to the river Ganga, it is only thrown into it. In the North-Western Provinces some cut off a bit of the cartilege of the right ear of the animal and then set it free. Such an animal is never touched by a good Hindu. Many animals consecrated to the gods are let loose without any mutilation, but such animals are marked by some distinguishing signs such as a collar &c.

Young calves are branded with the marks of a discus at the poles of whose rectitudinally intersecting diameters are attached the trident, such calves are held sacred and the branding of calves in sacrifices is considered meritorious. The Vrshotsarga or the consecration of a Vrsha or bull is an ancient ceremony, and it is held to be specially necessary for the salvation of the soul of the departed. The Sastras say, many sons are desirable, for one of them may visit Gaya (to offer the pinda or cake) to the manes of the departed, or perform the Asvamedha (the horse sacrifice) or dedicate or consecrate a Nilavrsha a blue bull (Nilgao,) (Proc. A. S. B. 1868. p. 235). In those days when beef was an acceptable food of the Hindus the branding of bull with four cows and then letting them loose was evidently done with a view for the preservation of the species. In sacrificing an animal before an idol supposed to be eternal, such as the goddess Kali of Kalighata, no mantras need be repeated, the mere slaying of the sacrificial animal before the idol is quite sufficient. The meat however is afterwards cooked and then offered to the goddess.

The buffalo sacrifice should nowhere be made without an archana. The preliminaries of a buffalo sacrifice are the same as those of the goat except the prayer, which differs. The buffalo sacrifice is offered to the Bhairavi manifestation of Sakti in the same way as the Sandhya puja is made of Chamunda manifestation. The lord of buffalo is Yama, and it is consecrated with the mantra, Om as you bear' Devi Chandica and also contest with her, so subdue my enemies and bear me happily. You are bearer of Yama, you are most noble and imperishable. Grant me life, wealth and renown, oh Kasara I bow to you.

The subjoined is a figure of the sacrificial pillar.

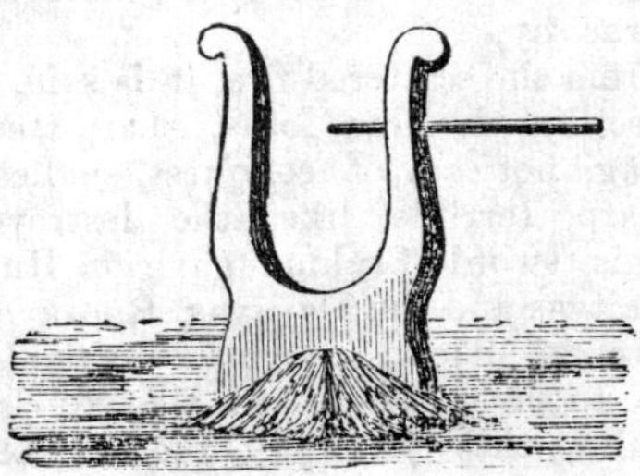

SACRIFICIAL PILLAR.

It is fixed on the ground and the neck of the animal is yoked on it. The Y-shaped post is generally made of red sandal wood, and it is securely fixed in the courtyard facing the pratima. The sword with which the sacrificial animal is despatched is a peculiarly formed instrument. The subjoined is a rough sketch of a sacrificial sword :

Sacrificial Sword.

In the archana of the sacrificial animal a hymn from the Vedas is recited in which it is stated that the gods were animals. In the Chaturhotra Chiti the several limbs of the sacrificial animals are identified with several gods. Om the sun is thine eye, Vayu thy life, the sky thy back.

The Khadga or the sacrificial sword is said to have been begotten by Brahma from his sacrificial fire. Though iron repeatedly occurs in the Vedas, it is interesting to note that no iron-sword was used in ancient days for making sacrifices. A wooden sword-like instrument called Sphya is stated to have been used for the several Vaidic sacrifices.

The sastras say,

" Then from the scattered fire, it is said, arose the sword, azure like the blue lotus, sharp-teethed, thin-waisted, long, not easy of conquest, endlessly bright, rustless, sharp, terrible like the destroyer of the world. This sword Brahma gave to Rudra to destroy the Daityas and the Danavas, Rudra again gave it to Vishnu to defend religion, Vishnu gave it to Marichi, he to the great Rshis, they to Indra, he to the Lokapalas, they to Manu the son of the sun, he to Ikshaku, he to Puroravas, he to Bhumisara, he to Bharat, he to Idavida, he to Dhundhumara, he to Kamboja, he to Muchakunda, he to Marut, he to Ushinara, he to Bhoja, he to Siva, he to Pratardana, he to Ashtakar, he to Rshadasva, he to Bharadvaja, he to Drona, he to Krpa, and he to the Pandus."

(45.) The Yoginis are the associate goddesses of Bhagavati, they are ten millions in number, but the following are the principal sixty-five mentioned in the Vrhannandikesvara Purana :

Narayani, Gauri, Sakambhari, Bhima, Raktadantica, Bhramari, Parvati, Durga, Katyayani, Mahadevi, Chandaghanta, Mahavidya, Mahatapa, Savitri, Brahmavadini, Bhadrakali, Visalakshi, Rudrani, Krshna, Pingala, Agnijvala, Raudramukhi, Kalaratri. Tapasvini, Meghasvana, Sahasrakshi, Vishnumaya, Jalodari, Mahodari, Muktakesi, Ghorarupa. Mahavayu, Sruti, Smrti, Dhiti, Tushti, Pushti, Medha, Vidya Lakshmi, Sarasvati, Aparna, Amvica, Yogini, Dakini, Sakini, Hakini, Nakini, Lakini, Tridasesvari, Mahashashthi, Sarvamangala, Lajja, Kausiki, Brahmani, Mahesvari, Kaumari, Vaishnavi, Aindri, Narasinhi, Varahi, Chamunda, Sivaduti, Vishnumaya, and Matrica. The first 30 are the attributes and different names of the goddess Sakti, the next eleven are the manifestations of force in the mental world, the next seven are the spirits which abide in the region of the dead and now and then visit the world of the living on special errands and the remaining, the female manifestations of the several gods Indra &c.

---

(46) A virgin Brahmani as well as a Brahmani wife are held in great esteem, by the Hindus, and they are

both worshipped as Prakrti, the female producing agency. The Brahmani wife or the Sadhava is worshipped by a Brahmana as well as the Virgin Brahmani and the worship is held important in the Durga puja as Durga herself is considered a Virgin (Virgo ?). The Kumari puja is performed after the arati, in the forenoon which follows animal sacrifice, and it is completed by offering betel-leaves to the brahmani girl. The articles ordinarily offered to her are the arghya, the padya (water for washing the feet), oil and turmeric, the dhupaincense, the lamp, water for bathing, cosmetics, virmilion, alaktaka, a mirror, and a toilet basket containing pomade, ribbons, a comb, pins, a necklace, a virmilion paste pot, also eatables, vestments, flowers and a garland.

(47.) The Matris are Brahmani, Mahesvari Kaumari, Vishnavi, Varahi, Indrani, Jogisvari, Kapalamalini, Chamunda, Sri, and Yakshini.

Brahmani is like Brahma four-faced, four-armed seated on a goose and holding in two hands the beads and in the other two the Kamandula or sacrificial vase. Mahesvari is like Mahesvara, adorned with braided locks and a helmet, seated on a bull and bearing a crescent moon on the forehead and holding in three hands a human skull, a spear, and a club, and blessing with the fourth. Kaumari is like Kumara seated on a beautiful peacock, dressed in red clothes and like him holding in two hands a lance and a spear. Vaishnavi is like Vishnu seated on Garuda (the bird god) four-armed, and holding in three hands a discus, a conchshell, and a club and blessing with the fourth. Varahi is seated on a buffalo, she too is like Varaha holding a bell, a chauri, a mace and a discus, she is the destroyer of the prince of the Danavas. Indrani is like Indra holding the thunderbolt, a spear, and a club. The goddess is seated on an elephant and covered with many eyes. Her complexion is that of molten gold and she is adorned with ornaments of all descriptions. Yogisvari holds a sharp sword, she is long-tongued and her locks are erect : she bears a bone in her hand and has a fierce look from a terrible set of teeth, she is lean-stomached. Kapalamalini is adorned with a wreath of human skulls, she holds in her left hand a skull filled with flesh and blood and in her right her own locks with a weapon. She is seated on a vulture or a raven, she is stomachless, and fierce-faced and three-eyed. Chamunda holds a bell and elephant skin, the four quarters of the globe are her clothes, she is seated on an ass, and she is skull-wreathed, her ornaments consist of deep red flowers and she is decorated with a flag. Sri is young ; her checks are round and full, her lips are tinged with red, and her eyebrows curved, her breast high and compact, her ear ornamented with jewelled rings, her face is rounded, and her head is covered with beautiful locks of hair, her hands holding lotus flower and the svastica, and her body protected by a waistcoat, her bosom adorned with necklaces, her arms are like the round and tapering body of the snake, she is dressed in beautiful clothes and surrounded by lovely looking girls, busily engaged in fanning her with chauris, she is seated on a lotus, she is bathed by elephants with many kinds of vessels. Yakshini is surrounded by Siddhas and Asuras, in the praying mood, with ghatas filled with water on her sides and seated on a chair on the step of which rest gods, Danavas and Nagas, &c.

The Matris otherwise denominated Dhatris or nurses of the human frame, agents by means of which food is converted into force, are personified Karanas or organs of the body, represented by the letters of the alphabet, which on account of their symbolical character are sometimes regarded as Matris, prototypes being taken for their archetype. Ideas being expressed by words, and words being indicated by sounds, the sound is regarded to be the essence of thought. As the letters of the alphabet represent the sounds, they are regarded by a set of philosophers as the Matris or universal genetrices.

The Matris according to the Markandeya Purana are female personifications of the energies of the gods Brahma, Vishnu, Mahesa, Indra, Kumara &c., and are consequently denominated Brahmani, Vaishnavi &c., who joined with the increate energy of the Devi in her war with the Daityas, who durst invade the dominion of heaven and defy Brahma the first-born progeny of Narayana. The Varaha Purana gives an interesting account of the genesis of the Matris from Divine energies for the purpose of vanquishing the numerous hosts of Dragons, which incessantly sprang from every drop of blood spilt from the body of the demon Andhaka (Darkness) whom Siva killed with his trident. The Raktavijas or blood-springing demons of the Hindus have their equivalents in teeth-springing demons of Cadmus on the shores of Greece. The philosophy of this worship seems to be the adoration of the Energy, which reduced the brute sounds of primitive man to the speaking language of man as a thinking animal. The Matris are divided into three classes of Antar, Vahya and Sanhara Matris *i. e.* internal, external and destructive or contracting. The Antarmatris are represented in a metaphysical narrative of the above-named Purana as allegorical prosopopœa of the eight principal passions or secondary powers or principles or motives of action of ethical writers, originating from the energies (*exergasia*) of superior powers and faculties and giving a continuous impetus to humane activity. They are eight in number, and are reckoned in the following order :—

1st.—Yogesvari the goddess of concupiscence, cohabitiveness, formed of a flame issuing from the breast of Siva (Jove). 2nd Rudrani, Fury springing from Rudra (rage) or Mahesvara the great Osiris. 3rd Vaishnavi the goddess of vassalage, cupidity and covetousness, arising from Vishnu. 4th Brahmani representative of *mada* (madness) another name for pride, proceeding from Brahman, the god of greatness. 5th Kaumari, Virginity, ignorance and nudity, primitiveness and the sustainer of the Rig Veda, female form of combativeness otherwise called ignorance, derived from Kumara the god of youth and valour. 6th Indrani, representation of envy springing from Indra the god of ambition. 7th Yami, female form of malice, sprung yama the regent of death. 8th Varahi the goddess of calumny, proceeding from Varaha incarnation of the gory boar.

The Matricas reside in conjunction with their male agents in the system of the six spheres and the two higher regions of the human body enumerated in Shat-chakra, *Vide* Bhuṭasuddhi.

The fifty letters of the Hindu alphabet represent as many deities residing in various interior parts of the body. Their local relations and particular functions are summed up in the eight spheres mentioned in Note 20. For further particulars see the Ekakshari Kosha and the Tantras.

According to another authority there are sixteen Matris, which are different attributes, corporeal and intellectual, deemed necessary for the integrity of the body and soul. These are Gauri (Brigetta), Sachi (Katharina), Padma (Nymphœa), Medha (Memoria), Savitri (Eleanora), Vijaya (Nicolœa), Jaya (Victoria), Devasena (Bellona), Svaha, Svadha, Santi (Rosamunda), Pushti (Rebecca), Dhrti (Patientia), Tushti (Beatrix), Atmadevata and Kuladevata.

(48.) The Nayikas are attendant energies of Durga Sakti. They are eight in number and appear to be verbal modifications of the manifestation of Chanda. They are thus worshipped on the Ashtami and Navami days in the mystic circular lotus-formed yantra (see Note 56): "Om you are most respected and you defeat every body, you reside like a bird, in the forelock, in space, and in the world, do you descent on this circle" Then follows the worship, of each of the Nayikas. I. Urgrachanda (Violent Chanda) is invoked and worshipped on the eastern petal of the lotus ; Hrim Srim to Urgrachanda. She is described as red coloured, sixteen armed, decorated with many ornaments, bearing wonderful garlands and dressed in variegated clothes and holding many weapons in her hands. Om obeisance to Ugrachanda, the destroyer of the demon Chanda. Do you bless us in the form of Chanda O Devi. II. Prachanda is invoked on the south-eastern petal of the lotus. She is saffron coloured and fourteen-armed variously ornamented and armed with several weapons. Om Prachanda ! Do you always bless us with children and preside over the Prachandaganas &c. III. Chandogra (Chanda the Violent) is said to be black coloured and twelve armed residing in the southern petal of the lotus. Om you are the sustainer of all existences and the defender of all beings &c., Chandogra has the particle Ugra (violent) placed after the name. IV. Chandanayika (emphatically *the* Nayika or Sakti of Chanda) is invoked on the south-western petal of the lotus. She is described as blue coloured, sixteen-armed and holding a skull, a shield, a bell, a mirror, a bow, a flag, a noose, a spear, a club, a lance, a thunderbolt, a sword, a goad, an arrow, a discus and a javelin. V. Chanda is invoked on the western petal of the lotus. She is said to be white coloured and eight armed. VI. Chandavati pertaining to Chanda is invoked on the north-western petal of the lotus. She is brown coloured and six-armed. VII. Chandarupa (Chanda-formed) is invoked on the northern petal of the lotus. She is red coloured and four-armed. VIII. Atichandika (great Chandi) is invoked on the north-eastern petal of the lotus. She is black coloured and four armed, bearing a conchshell, a discus, a mace and a lotus flower. Rudrachanda is invoked in the pericarp.

The above are the Nayikas of Sakti but there are according to the Sastras Nayikas or female attributes of nine other gods.

(49.) THE Vatukas are infantine manifestations of Siva and as such are not quite so ferocious as the Rudras and the Bhairavas. Vatuka literally means a boy. The Vatukas are therefore young manifestations of the several gods, thus we have Brahmaniputra the son of Brahmani, Mahesvariputra the son of Mahesvari &c. Besides these there are Vatukas who are sons of Dakinis, Rakinis, Lakinis, Kakinis, Sakinis, Hakinis, and Malinis. Their form is said to be three-fold according to the class of worshippers. They are mild-formed for the sattika (sincere, spontaneous or secular) worshippers, less mild-formed, the Rajasa (showy ostentatious, pure, civil or political) for the Rajasa worshipper and awfully terrific for the Tamasa (perverted ignorant, demoniac or diabolical) worshippers.

(50.) Pitha literally means a seat, a carpet, and as the Sastras enumerate seats of certain metals, wood and crystals as auspicious for certain ceremonies we have silver seats, gold seats, crystal seats, jewelled seats &c. The seat of Durga being the back of the lion standing on a jewelled platform, in the Pitha Nyasa therefore the jewelled seat is said to have claw or teeth as hard as the thunderbolt. But according to the Sastras, Pithas are holy places where the several parts of the corpse of Sati, the daughter of Daksha and wife of Siva, severed by Vishnu with his discus, had fallen. They are fifty-one in number. The Kalighata and the Kamakhya Pithas are much respected by the Hindus of Bengal.

(51.) THE titular deities are numerous. Annapurna and Visalakshi are in Benares, Lingadharini in Naimisha, Lalita in Prayaga (Allahabad), Gandhesvari in Gandhamadana hill, Rukshmini in Dvaraka, Radhica in Vrndavana, Kshemankari in the Madhyadesa (central provinces), Durga in Jambu Dvipa, &c. They are manifestations of Sakti and some of them are also Pitha deities.

(52.) THE Saktis alluded to here are different from the other manifestations of force or energy. They are three in number, Victoria, Berenice, and Omnia. These are the Saktis or attributes of Durga who is represented as destroying the demon. J. A. S. B. Vol. XXXIX. part I. p. 201.

(53.) THE weapons of Durga are each separately invoked and worshipped. The weapons have been deified and adoration is paid to them in the following manner.

1. Khadga, the sword. (Gladius,) Om to Isa! thou art chastiser sharp-edged, invincible, producer of fortune, victorious, and the defender of the faith, I bow to thee.

The text has Srigarbha for the 'producer of fortune.' Srigarbha is a compound word, Sri means prosperity and garbha womb, *i. e.*, one whose womb contains Sri or prosperity. Is it because the sword is the genetrix of fortune or wealth as steel is said to be the "acquirer of gold,"or because the curve of the sacrificial sword is like the vowel sign of ঈ in শ্রী ?

2.—Om Trident tri-regionis-benefactor! thou art the destroyer of all our foes, give us thy blessing.

3.—Om Discus, thou art a form of Vishnu ever residing in Vishnu's palm as well as in that of Devi, obeisance to thee oh good-looking circus!

4.—Om Arrow, thou art the best of all missiles and the subduer of the demoniac forces, defend us from all quarters, obeisance to thee.

5.—Om Sakti (javelin) the weapon of the gods and specially of Kartikeya protect us everywhere in thy missile form.

6.—Om Khetaka in thy club-like form destroy the enemy; located in Devi's palms always protect us.

7.—Om Bow propeller of great weapons, and destroyer of the enemies of gods, defend us everywhere and continue to be a bestower of blessing on us.

8.—Om Serpentine-noose, venomous and full of poison, ever unbearable to thine enemy, obeisance to thee.

9.—Om Goad, governor of elephants, for the defence of the worlds thou art placed in Parvati's palm.

Om Shield oppose the glory of the enemy in battle and defend me, for I am thy protege, obeisance to the hide-bodied.

10.—Om the Bell, thou depressest the valour of the enemy by the world-wide ring, purify us for ever from our iniquities.

Om Axe victorious over the enemy of the gods, I bow to thee the annihilator of our adversaries.

---

(54) The Kshetrapalas are as the name implies lords of the field. They are said to preside over the different parts of a cultivated field, and as such they are worshipped with Indra and other gods. In the Panchatantra the serpent is described to be one of the lords of the field as are the rats and other animals which obstruct the growth of paddy. In the Tantras however the Kshetrapalas are the masculine attendants of the Matrikas, and they are therefore as many in number as there are letters of the alphabet, Vide Note 47. The latter Kshetrapalas (Lares?) appear to have been derived from kshetra the womb, and hence their relation with the Matrikas with whom they are worshipped in the accouchment room. Petronius says "the youth having entered into Trimalcion's Banqueting-Hall, clad in white Tunicks, placed the

gods Lares upon the table adorned with *Bullæ.*" The Matrikas are fifty in number, but as the last letter क्ष of the alphabet stands for the collective kshetrapalas, there are left only forty-nine letters to be presided over by them. The initials of the names of the kshetrapalas are formed by each letter of the alphabet, thus we have Ajara, Apakumbha, Indrastuti, Idachara, Uktasanjna, Unmada, Rshisudana, Rmukta, Lptakesa, Lpaka, Ekadanshtraka, Airavata, Oghavandho, Aushadhisa, Anana, Astravara, Kavala, Kharukhanala, Gamukhya, Ghantada &c. &c.

In the Durgotsava eight Kshetrapalas are invoked, they are evidently of the Tantric group *i. e.* titular deities of the field.

(55.) THE Dikpalas are lords of the eight points of the compass and of the upper and lower regions. They are the well known gods Siva, Surya, Indra, Agni &c., but they are worshipped as Dikpalas inasmuch as they are located in the points above mentioned. Indra, the Sun, the Phases of the Moon, the Asterism, the Conjunctions, and the Karanas preside over the east; Agni, Hari, Sukra (Venus), Ganesa over the south east; Rahu and Ketu (the nodes) over the south; the cruel Kshetrapala over the south-west; Varuna, Garuda and the Rshis over the west; the Vasus, Cupid, the Seasons, Vayu and the Moon over the north-west; Kuvera, the Hills, the Earth and the Learned over the north; and Isana and the Gurus over the north-east.

(56.) SARVATOBHADRA is a symmetrical figure. It is described with coloured powders. It consists of a square in the geometrical centre of which is drawn eight-petalled white lotus, the interstices between the petals being painted black. The pericarp is marked yellow, and the anthers are distinguished by alternate streaks of red, black and yellow.

This lotus is enclosed in a black circle interrupted by a band of red which forms the opening of the circle. The circle is encompassed by a yellow square, which is again enclosed in a larger red square. In the same line of the opening of the circle is formed a white band friezed yellow, connecting the small with the large square. This last square again is enclosed in three square zones of white, red and black color from within outwards. The opening of the second square from the centre is continued by a white band to the extremity.

The second square is variegated by red and white bands and the outer square by red, yellow and black, the last being placed in the corners and one white band in the middle of each side.

---

(57). ON the day of Navami after the sacrifice and Homa the priests are presented with their Dakshina or honourarium and the festival is considered at an end, and the gods are requested to depart. On the morning of Dasami, before the immersion in water, takes place the goddess is said to reside in the heaps of flowers which have been offered to the Devi and which lie near the Ghata. The Goddess who is supposed to reside in the Nirmalya or offals is said to be Chandalini or a low caste Goddess, and therefore the food offered to her is coarse aud rude and consists of flattened rice, confection of baked rice, and of the stalks of Colocasia antiquorum.

---

(58). THE auspicious articles are 1stly a broad dish called a Varanadala in which the following things are displayed, viz., clay, sandal wood, a pebble, paddy, durvagrass, flowers, fruits, curd, ghi, virmilion, a conchshell, collyrium, gorochana, mustard, gold, silver, copper, a chauri, a mirror, a lamp, and turmeric, 2ndly a wicker husking fan on which are placed several painted earthen pots with lids and rice and cowries coloured yellow with turmeric, the fan being covered with a red piece of silk, 3rdly the Sri and Svastica described above, 4thly a Ghata filled with water. These are used in performing a varana or adhivasa of an idol and a bridegroom. Pots filled with water, plantain trees, twigs of mango and asoka, and wreaths made of mango leaves, asoka and nuts &c., are placed at the entrance of the hall of worship.

(59.) CORACCIAS INDICA and the brahmani kite are let loose on the occasion of depositing the pratima in water. The observance of such auguries is not peculiar to Durgotsava. The Sastras say that if one sees a corpse, a jackal and a ful-pot to the left, and a cow, a deer and a brahman to the right at his exit from home on some business errand his journey is attended with success. Again, if one sees or recollects or repeats the names of the following *viz.* a cow with her calf, a bull, an elephant, a horse, lighted fire on the right side, a handsome woman, a garland of flowers, a prince, a prostitute, a flag, fresh meat, ghi, curd, honey, silver, or white paddy he attains the object of his journey.
